In Memory
of
Elizabeth Seymour Rawlinson
Lover of Nature

1901   1942

The Augusta Garden Club

THIS BOOK

was created with the generous spirit and assistance of our corporate sponsors, whose passionate commitment to sustaining and improving the quality of life here in Albemarle speaks within these pages.

VIRGINIA NATIONAL BANK

KESWICK HALL AT MONTICELLO

McLEAN FAULCONER, INC. REALTORS

INDIVIDUAL SPONSORS ARE

A. Cary Brown, C. Wilson and Carter McNeely III, Dorothy Batten Rolph, Katherine Brooks, Margareta Douglas, Robert Strini, Jerome and Paula Beazley, Greg and Kim Briehl

ALBE

MARLE

A STORY OF LANDSCAPE AND AMERICAN IDENTITY

WORDS AVERY CHENOWETH   PHOTOGRAPHS ROBERT LLEWELLYN

IN THIS
LANDSCAPE, TO THE EAST OF THE BLUE RIDGE,
BETWEEN THE JAMES AND POTOMAC RIVERS. . .

THE S T I L L N E S S AND DISTANCE DRAW US TO
EACH OTHER IN A PRIMAL WAY.

THIS IS A LANDSCAPE WITH A HUMAN SCALE,

WHOSE VALLEYS FALL

INTO THE SHAPE OF ROOMS THAT WE MAY E N T E R.

The last hour of daylight burns softly on the porch, where the conversation between friends is intelligent and often hilarious, there

beneath the fan. We begin telling stories of how we wound up in this area. One of us is from California, two of us came to the University, and one of us grew up nearby. Wherever we may have come from, we have chosen to live here. The hosts say they came to this house almost on a whim, but one glance at the view and they never thought of living anywhere else. Upon hearing this, we turn, each of us, and take in the Blue Ridge at dusk. The landscape is a presence among us. The stillness and distance draw us to each other in a primal way not found amid the buffers of society, and our senses open to everything out there. Here is a depth before us, translucent with memory, blue in the early chill of autumn, and fresh with transition. This is the dream of philosophy, of finding for each of us a personal unified field theory in which our minds and hearts connect with the ineffable, and as the conversation rolls on into the night, we feel changed by the encounter, however momentary.

Here in a beautiful landscape, we experience the sublime. And yet this moment of life is one that we may lose in the thrum of daily living. The scene is easy to imagine. As we drive along, taking the kids to school, talking on the cell phone, or

13

thinking of what we have to do, we may fail to notice more than the world's flashing appearance outside the car. We may not know that we share with ancient people a love for the design and intimacy of the hills. It is the oldest story we have—when a certain Neolithic man senses in a beautiful landscape a spiritual presence, which he calls divine. The experience of communion with nature is a founding expression of the human spirit. And in this supple medium, we may find once again a few moments of transparency and transcendence.

In this landscape, to the east of the Blue Ridge, between the James and Potomac rivers, the terrain of the Piedmont floats like a casually thrown picnic blanket, and becomes for many a fabric that presents an inexhaustible cornucopia. The mystery and spirituality, indeed, even the romance, of this landscape is a force that changes those who give themselves to it, but which also resonates for everyone in its own harmonic field. And so it may not be surprising that so many people have chosen to be here—a flow of immigration now centuries old.

This book is an exploration of the almost invisible ways by which we have changed the land and the land has changed us. The land feeds us, and in long cycles of reciprocity, we nourish the land. The first garden of literature was full of flowering fruit trees, and although this formula has come down to us through the paradise gardens of Persia and India, we nonetheless nurture intuitive gardens in the places where we live. From the vast pattern of a landscape to the small enclosure behind the house, we blend the elements of water and flower and fruit into an atmosphere of spiritual intimacy. In this manner of taking care, we follow an ancient path into an emotional landscape where all things are in harmony. And yet the story that we found in the Albemarle landscape is one that expands into larger spaces alto-

15

gether. This landscape, which we believe is unique, encompasses our earliest ideas of America.

Throughout the hills and plains, we have written our story in the land itself, transforming it from a largely unbroken expanse of woods into an evolving landscape whose various features reflect the time and economy of those who managed to live here. Whether in the field and forest of the first Amerindians, who moved inside an organic balance of animals and climate, or in the ruinous early tobacco farms of the English, the story of our own self-creation is the story of how we have lived upon the surface of the planet. The past is alive around us everywhere, even if the expressions of our presence are worn into illegibility by centuries of weather and construction, and lost to us by our own collective illiteracy as we wander through this colossal invisible library. The unexplored culture of our landscape is about the received and hidden monuments we have made for others and ourselves. From the Ice Age to the present, the Monacans to the Moderns, people have shaped this land to carry on the deep continuity of the human story in this world. And we have in the land around us ideas—religious, aesthetic and philosophical—that we can trace through these woods halfway around the planet, to ranges and rivers none of us have seen.

They are ideas whose arc passes from antiquity, across the moment, and into the future. For the Albemarle landscape we have is driven by more than harmony; these lands are scored by the curiosity of a scientific age, and by a Colonial will for self-determination. As with many stories, a few distinct personalities come into the foreground, where they stand with a breadth of shoulder and cast a shadow into our time.

He was an adolescent when his fascination for Native Americans and natural history came alive in the forest near his

family farm in Shadwell. And he was in his first term of the Presidency when his passion to discover what lay out beyond the Louisiana Territory led him to send the Corps of Discovery, under Lewis and Clark, into a vast and undiscovered country. Although Thomas Jefferson is known more as the author of the Declaration of Independence, in which we hold received truths to be self-evident, he is also the author of our idea that we are entitled to the pursuit of happiness. Here is a clause devoted to releasing imagination in abundance, energy and the will to self-determination that have separated the United States, as a nation founded upon our own secular ideology, from other nations founded upon the exclusionary ideas of tribal unity. This pursuit of an elusive and scarcely understood ideal of happiness has driven—or recognized—in our national character a passion for an endless frontier, whether in the material or the metaphorical. The unknown place has moved from the Northwest Passage in Jefferson's administration, literally to the moon in the Kennedy administration, and will continue on into explorations that we cannot imagine. We see this idea at work in Jefferson's own invented way of life, at play in our own passion for individualism, if not idiosyncrasy, and in the allure to so many from around the world, who come here to reinvent themselves. Nations driven by the hegemony of the tribe are about the past; those given to the promise of the individual are about the future. And while he may have settled anywhere, he chose instead to return and build his university here, in spite of opposition. His ideas, inspired by the landscape around him, have come to us without any loss of force, and we can still look at that view of the mountains under an August moon and sense the mystery. In this curious sense, he is never more than a chair away, there on the porch beside us.

The first June evening in the country,

as we began, our intention was to create a book that would capture the essence of the place where we live. And we met with open doors and enthusiasm along our travels, which throughout the seasons carried us down each of the more than seven hundred roads in Albemarle County, and slightly beyond. The reason for such a hale greeting is that we all feel a connection to this place; we all have our story of how we came here and why, and we often hear a call to come to this landscape. More than record images of our land as we see it around us, though, we also wanted to show the landscape that so many conscientious people are placing under conservation easement. A green thread of protected land braids throughout the images. This land will remain far from the public view once it is protected from development. And so one of our desires was to capture the hidden Albemarle, the one most of us will never see.

On our drives, we have seen meadows and mountains, vineyards and lost roads—one such road braced between stone walls may date back before the Revolution. We have gone sloshing up the liquid hillside of Applebury Road, and gone surfing down again on four wheels. We have seen the expanse of wealth, the collected magnificence of fortunes, and the ramshackle collapse of third-world poverty encircled by a Stonehenge of automobiles. In places that were perhaps the villages of Monacan Indians for thousands of years, we have seen boys and girls playing soccer. We have rolled through neighborhoods whose road names are those of the Indian tribes now vanished, and whose architecture reflects the modern enthusiasm for the car and conformity. We have trod lightly across eighty-foot wide beaver dams only to step carefully if accidentally off into freezing water, hip-high, with cameras high overhead. With the sound of traffic roaring through the trees, we have come to the sacred sites of the Monacan Indians, and are standing, without knowing it, near the place of a secret enclave, one of many, where freed Africans once also lived—safely away from whites.

Through the cold and spacious woods of October, we stumbled around until our guide found the lost graveyard of slaves that she had told us about, a scattering of small headstones mixed among the trees. Not far away, upon a hilltop and thickly ingrown, was another graveyard she showed us, this one bearing the monuments of a once prominent colonial family, all the variance between the owned and the owning having been subsumed in the everlasting embrace. We have found our way and gotten lost, and have done both only to have an image call out to one or both of us. One evening, after some bragging about my sense of direction, we found ourselves lost in the weaving pattern of carriage paths on a great estate, thanks to my confusion. Bob stopped the car and hopped out. An image had called out to him, and there in the near dark of an autumn evening, he captured one of the more intricate images of beauty we have ever seen—a pattern of iridescent yellow leaves on glossy dark.

In a landscape like ours, which began as a frontier, people have come for an intangible something and then moved on, for centuries. Their stories are as individual as a person, as collective as a generation, and often eloquent of an entire age, but they each involve a search, the leaving and arriving in mass which began long before the American era. Everyone we met with had a story to tell about how he or she came to live here. One woman told us that she came here because the life in Los Angeles had become harrowing, and she had to return to a place whose landscape is spiritually inspiring. She expressed a theme

we often heard, and one that we could relate to, as well. This is a book about transformations, and the first time I ever felt the allure of this place was in the rapidly morphing Sixties.

Every summer before the birth of

the interstates, my father would throw us into the back of the car, and take us on a yammering 18 hour drive from central New Jersey down to the southeast corner of Tennessee, where we would summer amid clamor, corn pone, and cousins. For many years this journey was dreadful, and there were times when my siblings and I would be sucked up against the windows, gasping for oxygen.

In the years we spent caged in the back of the Buick Skylark—before videos invaded the family space of the station wagon—we would suffer from mind-cracking boredom. The small distractions of counting license plates or stopping to walk the dog or retie the luggage to the roof were only entertaining for so long. Soon we would simply gaze at the landscape. And to our surprise, we began seeing things in it. We were able to read its moments: the waves of rolling grass, the gateless meadows, the cow-dotted lows and highs, the sere clouds and tawny hillsides. This wasn't the suburbs, this was agriculture—something we had glimpsed on a Saturday show at sunrise called *The Modern Farmer*. But there it was, right out there, and people really did live like that—and there was a kid riding a tractor who was our age.

In the fields and in their pattern of unfolding—especially when moving at the speed of exasperation—you felt a kind of compression, something as wonderfully suggestive as a story told at bedtime in a strange house. You knew by some handprint of light and shadow, which gave shape to the hills, where we

were and where we were going, and you knew this was about more than the next fast food restaurant. Throughout those years, summer, pale and hot, would breeze by to the melodies of "Touch Me," "Wedding Bell Blues," and other pop confections. An ineffable sense of place would arise from the incidental commingling of youth and music and longing, and resolve before me outside the window, in a moving frame of farmland and small highway. From the first, then, a diffusion of American culture was informing a sense of the landscape.

The hillsides from Manassas to Charlottesville were among the most memorable, back in those impressionable years, when the route south of Washington meant leaving behind the media belt. You could feel the change of place keenly then, when you crossed the beltway, and left behind the howling national urgency and slipped into the regional lack of concern. The Top 40 music of New York would die away against the twang and lament of country music, and the naive longing would now be voiced in small-town scandal. Local accents would play on your ear with a shock of just how different the United States was way out here, how empty and enormous. In New Jersey, the gas station guys would say, "Yeah? Dat'll be twenny dollas," with an edge so surly it was almost threatening. When we stopped in Warrenton we would hear, "Yes, Ma'am? What'll it be?" delivered with a rural skitter you never heard on TV and which has been vanishing since. And, the really weird part was, he was pleasant. Cordial even, as if we were on the church steps. The masculine hands, which jacked the pump into the car, were as gnarled as a Piedmont accent. But there was something else moving elusively around him in the summer buzz of neon. The distinctions of his region and speech, manner and pace, made him strangely authentic, as if he were from an actual place and we were from television.

And then came the first view of the continent. You can see it still, a moment north of Culpeper when Route 29 swings open and a north-to-south view of the Blue Ridge booms along the entire horizon in a single abstraction. Although the mountains are distinctly themselves, they are also diffuse enough to rise into icons of everything in the desire to go west, and this is the first call you hear. The mountains fade away in planes of color back toward some primal promise that fills you with an exhilaration of seeing all this...this... Wow! And other amplifiers you cannot find or apply because you are too young to field the experience. This swoon carries you almost above your bossy little sister, but rather than remain in the car, you meditate into the twilight until you slip once again into that sensation aroused by the disappearing view of dusk in the mountains.

This half-forgotten experience reawakened my interest in the area one summer when I was on a road trip. Until then, I had stared out the station wagon for decades as we zoomed around Charlottesville on Route 250 and had wondered what went on amid the cluster of rooftops in the trees; and always a voice told me that *she* would be waiting here, whoever *she* was. And so, one year, rather than sweep around and head north, I turned off 250 and found my brother's cottage on 15th Street. I parked, got out, looked around, have stayed for 10 years—and have always felt the continuum. The atmosphere that afternoon was a blend between Hopper and Di Chirico: the emptiness of the summer street; the sense of a small town away from the noise; the way light cast spangles in the leaves and sent long sloping shadows across the University grounds. I sat in a deli with a glass of beer, watching the students in the twilight: all of this had for me the conviction of finding a place where life could be different than it had been up north, back when I worked inside the Media Belt.

The town with its southern sleepiness was a reason to park, but the allure of beauty was again reason to drive; and listening to the eloquence of the landscape was soon a theme for years of weekend touring without a destination, much less a map. Even for a novice, something may happen out there between you and the land, whether you have gotten out to wander, to enjoy a romantic picnic, or merely to pause and gaze at the scenery. In time, you may wonder, What is it about the perception of beauty that gives rise to a sense of the divine? There, between you and the land, is a floating interstice that fills with a volume of light, tonic as music, and perceptible as stars on the periphery of your vision. How or why does such a thing happen; how do these mountains create such an epiphany? Are they as self-selecting as ghosts, seen only by those who want to? Is some biochemistry at work in the brain's reaction to a light field without depth? Is there some magnetic anomaly that underlies this land, just as the largest known vein of soap stone runs between Scottsville and Charlottesville—and can these effects be measured, like radioactivity? Are we sensing something tangible, or is this an awareness of our senses working?

The answers would lie between the nature of inspiration, and the inspiration of nature.

After this awakening to the world

outside the car, the landscape began to appear everywhere, and its omnipresence in art and TV taught you how to see. In the bottom of a china dish, for example, you could gaze into the tiny scene of a brook with a bridge, a cottage, a flock of sheep and a shepherd. Right there, between the corn on the

cob and the fried chicken, there were little people living in a story book world. And there it was again on the wall of an Edwardian house, a view of paradise grown obscure beneath a surface of varnish whose dry cracks were like the papery skin on a great-grandmother's fragile hands. Yet beneath the feathery trees was a scene of paradise. And there they were again, from central casting, the barefoot boy with cheeks of tan, his flock of sheep, and an alluring view of promise deepening into the sunset beyond a fold in the mountains. Sometimes such images would recall a flash of the original experience: Natural Bridge, where we gaped in awe; or a weird nowhere would flit by in cartoons. Whether in a dish or in a painting, in figured wall paper, or in a carved headboard with bunches of apples and grapes, the theme was invariably that of bountiful paradise, a world unknown to anyone living, perhaps, but felt in a spiritual sense and composed in bucolic harmony. Our view of the landscape is tinted by an aesthetic lens, seen or unseen.

The purpose to which we put the land will also define the land we see. While one man may see the farm where his grandfather grew up, another may see a parcel where he wants to build a shopping center on top of all those Norman Rockwell memories. An accountant may see a write off, disguised as a cattle operation, while an insect scientist may see a world of seething micro-violence. So, why is Albemarle so appealing to so many? Why this place and these mountains? My guess is that the snowy ranges out west are so severe and geologic, so primal and timeless, that they render tiny and vulnerable the humid creatures blinking at them. The western mountains, youthful and energetic, are about dinosaurs and volcanoes; the story of evolution; the terrifying existentialism of prehistory carved in layers of rock and exposed in the skeleton-beds of behemoths. This is the Ozymandias syndrome: behold my mighty works and tremble, say the bones of a T-Rex. The Rockies are about the past because, paradoxically, they are so new that we can read the past in them. The mountains of this area are so much older that, paradoxically, they are about the present because we can see ourselves in them. The Southwest Mountains, which roll on a southwest line from Fredericksburg to Monticello, are the American Himalayas. Long before the Rockies began itching to climb, these mountains were a vaulting continental range beneath which were the explosions and thunder of a primordial ocean. Now in their dotage, they are worn so small that they can be driven over in about 15 minutes. Rather than diminish our presence, though, they inspire more expansive feelings altogether. And in this feeling of immediacy we found another recurring theme, in conversation.

In some ways the appeal of this area seems to lie in its reassurances. This is a landscape with a human scale, whose valleys fall into the shape of rooms that we may enter and enjoy in privacy, and whose visible husbandry conveys a sense of purpose and control. We feel safe here. The pattern of white fences, or of trees along a creek, enhances for the human eye this sense of personal scale so that we are not overawed by the enormous surround, but entranced. And while this may be our own preferred lens for visualizing the landscape and relating its story, we have a tradition of felt presence here in these hills that long predates the Judeo-Christian tradition. Our beliefs and visions, especially in the media age, drop a semi-transparent screen that separates us from the landscape even as it inspires us. What we have done in this book is to try and capture the landscape we have come to know as our home, and do so while examining the various lenses of perception, on camera and in culture. We have tried to *see* the spirit that is alive here.

Lenses on or off, we met many different people, migrants to millionaires, in our year of travelling the myriad parts of this

county. From roadsides to boardrooms, we have many people to thank, farmers and environmentalists, and others of a more spiritual or historical bent altogether. To make a book like this one involves a passionate and visionary community, and our hope is that this wide collaboration will tell unforeseen generations something about who we are, and what we cared so fervently about, that we saved it for them in these pages.

The sun has gone down behind

the Blue Ridge, creating that familiar awareness of other lives going on somewhere in the distant radiance. The air is damp and gold on the Queen Anne's lace and orchard grass, and permeates the evening with a thrill of change in the leaves, the smell of hay and of cattle. A few last points of sun fire in the tall grass and gleam along the white fence as it runs to cover amid the woods. The conversation picks up again, filling the pastures with our talk, but the vacant chair is not empty. The mountains and the moon create a scene that is out of time, heightening an awareness of our mystery, on a planet, under a moon, travelling in an outer band of the Milky Way. We come to the landscape to relive this first experience, to reawaken in ourselves a sense of what is vital and ineffable, to find a larger sense of where and who we are. The landscape has a voice of its own, an immense and subtle presence that compels in all of us an aesthetic wonder. A moment must be shared. The encounter makes us feel just how miraculous and inexplicable and brief all of this is for us, and the desire to know and enjoy all of it through our hearts is almost as sensuous as the lover's waist under your hand.

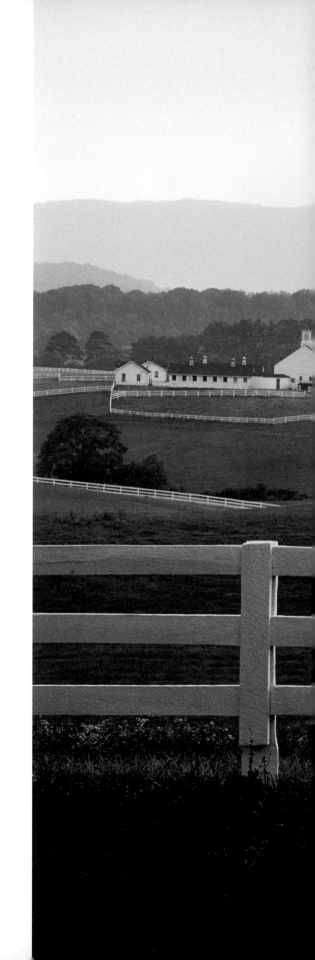

HERE IS A DEPTH BEFORE US,

TRANSLUCENT WITH MEMORY, BLUE IN THE CHILL OF AUTUMN, AND FRESH WITH

TRANSITION.

1

Not long ago, on a flood plain in northern Albemarle, a middle-aged man was exploring along a creek known as Blue Run, when two shards of stone called out to him from the ground next to his boots. He lifted the pieces and kept them, and they opened unforeseeable doors into an ancient world. The arrowheads convey a narrative of astonishing continuity for the Native people who once lived throughout this area of the Piedmont, and tell something as well of what happened to them.

They were the Monacans and their ambulatory circle of villages lay on a rolling path throughout the hills of Albemarle and beyond, including the larger expanse of the surrounding counties. Although we know little about them, we do know that Captain John Smith captured and interviewed one of their men in 1608, and that they were already leaving when the first English arrived in the Albemarle area almost a hundred years later. Even so, the evidence of their tools and villages, and the constancy of place and manufacture, are eloquent on their behalf. It's likely that their ancestors were among the first immigrants who came to this area, as far back as 12,500 years ago, when this environment was morphing through the centuries from the great forests follow-

ing the Ice Age, into the modern woodlands of today.

One of the arrowheads found that day is a Clarksville, a tiny triangle fashioned for killing birds, hunting and war. As a type, the Clarksville is the last of its kind, the final evolution of a style. They were made sometime in the 1600s, before the Native Americans adopted the imported technology of gunpowder weaponry. On the ground beside it was the second arrowhead, which turned out to be a distant cousin. Even though the two arrowheads may appear similar to an uninformed eye, they are not. The second tip is a style known as a Lecroy, which has been carbon-dated to a period of 6,500 to 8,000 years ago B.C.E. These two thin pieces of evidence held between the fingers, and no larger than a finger nail, together frame a span of time of as much as 10,000 years across, a canyon so wide that almost the entire sum of Western History fits inside. On the afternoon that the older arrowhead was chipped into existence, in about ten minutes, perhaps, the Roman Empire would have been science fiction set thousands of years into the future. The vast collectivity of humanity, the humming global hive of corporate and political organization in which we find ourselves buzzing, was further away from them, in that hour before the hunt, than the ice-age culture of their ancestors.

The more recent arrowhead, the Clarksville, relates a different story—in time, environment, and historical position. When this arrowhead was made, sometime in the 1600s, the future was closer than any Monacan could have imagined. The day the delicate bird tip was fashioned, the American Empire stood less than a hundred years off; its breadth and depth were just becoming visible, and its arrival here would prove as unavoidable and cataclysmic for them as the ice shield had been for their ancestors. After so many centuries in which they had adapted to changes in climate and game, it was the arrival of the

33

Europeans that would prove insuperable, and prompt the Monacans to leave. And a significant reason for this resolution lay in the different relations the competing tribes had with the land, and the ways in which they would change it into something greater still, the landscape.

To push back forward to

the beginning of things, as we know and infer them to have been once upon a time, let us see the mist that hangs over a chilly morning in June. The place is here, of course, but the time is some 17,000 years ago. Naturally, what we know of did not exist, but neither did the *where* of it. Far more comprehensive than the absence of people back then, is the fact that our Environment was not here, either. All of the landscape that we warm to every day as the mild and mellow Piedmont was for 100,000 years an arctic terrain, a weather-heavy tundra of violent winters brightened by a few weeks of summer.

Not far away, to our north, stood the arctic rim itself in the form of the Laurentian ice sheet. This vast semi-continent of ice, a mile thick, flowed down from the North Pole. It ran a crushing path as far south as Kentucky, and rumbled north of the plains of Gettysburg before slouching off toward New York. This ice sheet, with its terminal moraine of sliding boulders, was a mass so utterly gigantic that, in concert with other sheets in Europe, it dominated global weather. The living ice cast over the Piedmont that gray and brilliance, the frost and dark of prehistory that we associate with a time of caves, an unlivable place where extreme temperatures would drop to as much as a hundred below. And yet from a view in these hills, the first people may have arrived and surveyed the new place.

34

They were the Paleoindians, one of the migrating tribes of modern humans whose DNA we share and which has been traced to a female who lived in Africa some 200,000 years ago. Our ancient parents may never have known each other; and the two animating rivers of genetic information that began with an Eve and Adam may have flowed into each other across a divide of thousands of years. Contrary to the idea of an isolated mythical couple in a garden, though, they were not alone. Throughout the mountains, rain forest and grasslands of Africa, as many as 20,000 other individuals were alive then although we derive from only one set of genetic parents.

Long before the Paleoindians came down along the ice sheet and into North America, their ancestors had been in motion for about 100,000 years as part of the African Diaspora, which led the first modern humans north through the Middle East and into fanning arcs throughout Europe and Asia. They are modern in the sense that we come from them, and not from one of their quasi-human competitors, the Neanderthals. Neanderthal DNA was separated out some 500,000 years earlier when they went out of Africa but wound up living in pockets of isolation far away from the genetic blending still underway. These two groups, archaic and modern, apparently co-existed for many thousands of years, in Europe and the Middle East. The Neanderthals finally vanished some 35,000 years ago, at the height of the Ice Age, even though they had adopted by then the tools and technology of their enlightened neighbors. The archeological evidence shows that they had little creativity or ingenuity, before the moderns came. They made their tools the same way, and passed them on without improvement or innovation, for hundreds of thousands of years. And yet we believe nevertheless that they had brains larger than ours, and were possessed of an intelligence that we would recognize. Scientists debate whether the archaic and modern humans had children. In spite of their possibly freakish appearance to one another, the groups may well have enjoyed sexual relations. Whatever the likelihood of their sex lives, though, Neanderthal DNA has never been found in the present gene pool. Yet we do believe that they were sentient, and felt the presence of the spiritual world. We infer this from the fact that they buried their dead and lay to rest with them an assortment of tools and ornaments. For many scientists this behavior reveals a belief in life after death. And so there may have been a moment, as well, when one generation saw the scarcity of their numbers and saw the imminence of their end.

The flow of modern humans from Africa into the north went on for more than 500,000 years. Author Steve Olson points out that the exodus was very likely not in the form of an organized march that we often imagine, drawing, perhaps, upon our own cultural memory of wagon trains going west. He believes it may have been more gradual. As more people arrived in one area, others left and moved on by another day's walk. Indeed, their migration may have been so gradual that—at 50 miles a generation—they didn't know they were moving.

When they arrived in the Americas is not precisely known, and though they seem to have crossed the Bering Strait, they may also have crossed the ice to Greenland and Newfoundland. The idea that a European foray may have coincided with an influx from Siberia has arisen from the discovery in the Algonquin people of an X haplotype, a genetic marker that occurs only in Europe and dates back in their lineage some 9,500 years. The controversy among professionals here entails the mystery of how the continent was peopled. And though many scientists see the answer in the three waves of Eurasian immigrants who came through Canada during periods of ice melt, others now believe that an aboriginal people may have been here even before the Paleoindians. The possibility that an indigenous people were here first is enhanced by the absence in Native American myths of any story dealing with migration. The question of how people came to be here was a popular speculation among Colonials, making this one of our earliest inquiries. Indeed, oral history may have begun with, Where are you from?

The presence of Paleoindians in Virginia is braced between stone points, a modern anchor against ancient ambiguity. These are the Clovis points, a style of Lanceolate spear, hefty in hand and roughly eight inches in length. These lance points create as much mystery, though, as they clear up. Through radiocarbon dating they have been traced to a point and time of origination in South America centuries before people could have come in from Siberia, and they then appear sequentially moving in a gradual export to North America. To enrich the mystery, the Clovis points may be kin to a style found in only one other place, among the ice-age sites of the Basque country, in Spain. Before vertigo sets in, what researchers find so tantalizing here are the hypothetical new story lines the Clovis stones point up. Perhaps the Atlantic, during the Ice Age, was so low in volume, that an early people in Europe were tempted to explore, thousands of years before the Eurasians followed the herds of mammoths through China and Siberia and on into Canada.

Whatever their homeland or compass of arrival, the presence of Paleoindians in Virginia appears between two dates that suggest they were here thousands of years after the Ice Age had come to a warm conclusion. This places them here in the late Pleistocene, sometime between 12,500 and 9,000 B.C.E., when the Piedmont was harsh but habitable nonetheless. That approx-

imation is based upon the radiocarbon dates of the earliest Clovis stone spearheads found here, and to resolve the ambiguity, many scientists prefer a median of 11,200 years ago to place the first Clovis people in Virginia. But suppose the dates were not set by stone spearheads. If we suppose instead that the stone tools are only part of the story, then it seems humans may have been here much earlier. One site in western Pennsylvania, the Meadowcraft rock shelter, has been radiocarbon dated at its deepest level of apparent habitation to more than 19,000 years ago. At one site outside Richmond, Virginia, small blades and scraping tools have been dated to 15,000 years of age. It seems that, if we look into bits of trash and land-use, imagining for a moment that the earliest people used only leather and wooden tools that didn't survive, then the presence of humans in the Mid-Atlantic may have coincided with the Ice Age, after all.

Had they arrived here some 17,000 years ago, then, they would have seen a landscape that we would not recognize. As the mist rose in the valleys on that chilly morning in June, they would have seen a wind-bedraggled and broken wilderness of stunted oak, breaches of grass with alpine flowers, and herds of animals.

The mountains shone with a brilliant snow pack. Musk ox bent their heads to crop the shoots. A pack of gray wolves ran their loping stride along the edge of the caribou herd, or perhaps that was a pack of dire wolves; though smaller of head, they were just as large and had more massive teeth, used for crushing skulls. The first people saw moose, buffalo and elk, modern animals we know. And they saw animals that we know through oral tradition and science, families of woolly mammoth lumbering shaggy and slumped, in slow formation through the wind. Twelve feet high at the shoulder and weighing as much as eight tons, they presented a challenge to the evolving means of

collective hunting. The first people would have caught on the wind that day the musk of yet another but somewhat smaller snow elephant, a herd of mastodon grazing in the distance yet within their ability to organize and kill.

The mammoth and mastodon were not the only huge game the Paleoindians would have found here. By the rivers, they would have found giant beaver, seven feet in length and protected by enormous teeth and tail; woolly sloths that stood twenty-feet tall. The presence of huge game would have alerted them to the danger of huge predators.

Ten thousand years ago they might have found themselves in a competition for game with terrifying opponents. These were the saber-toothed and scimitar cats whose range included this ecosystem, though their remains have been found in northern Virginia and eastern Tennessee. These two nightmare cats would have dominated any terrain. With a mass of more than 900 pounds, an alpha male sabertooth would have been almost twice the size of the modern African lion. A half-ton of cat with eight-inch tusks, used for presentation and suffocating death bites, the sabertooth might have used an ambush attack, while the scimitar, somewhat smaller and lighter, longer of leg, and with fangs half the length, may have been more adept at chasing. What the first people had most to contend with, though, was warmth, making an encampment with enough southern exposure to catch pools of sunlight.

And so, what they saw on this June morning 17,000 years ago, were not the limits of game, berries and shelter, but more likely, their abundance. Here was a place with a generous supply of water, with ice melt weeping down cheeks of stone, into creeks fresh with fish. In the hills and bottomland unfurling between the confluent streams of Albemarle, they would create a path of life their descendents would follow for more than 10,000 years.

They arrive and their time slips away. They come into focus, without question or fiction, some 12,500 years ago, on the outside, when most of the ancient points seem to have been cut and fashioned, and can be dated. These long, serrated points are the Lanceolate, and the largest of them, the Clovis, would have been used to kill animals like bear, moose, and caribou, though not the behemoths of the Ice Age. For by then, the ice sheet was melting back into Canada, and the weather from the Carolinas to the Mid-Atlantic was starting to warm. In the time when the Clovis people were certainly living here, Albemarle was no longer tundra. For the next few thousand years, imagine instead the sub-arctic terrain of Newfoundland. The changes in climate and environment were rising north through the centuries and inundating the coastal states with liquid new warmth. Seasons began to appear. The air became moist. The plants, trees, and animals sustained by the arctic environment for 100,000 years were suddenly facing in the space of a century the destruction of their ecosystem. Only one or two key species would have to go extinct to set off a cascade failure that would take out dozens of other species with them.

Why the glaciers began to melt is a mystery with as many explanations as there are points of light in the sky. Theories range from the accepted idea that a gradual new inclination of the earth's axis toward the sun set off the sudden warming, to another theory which proposes that the release of carbon dioxide through volcanic explosions percolated and retained warmth in the envelope of the atmosphere. Scientists know that there have been only two warm periods on earth while humans have been here, one of them at the start of our ascent into humanity, and the other one, right now. There have been only four ice ages, but for countless millions of years the earth was so remark-

ably warm that 30-foot skeletons of alligators have been discovered within 700 miles of the North Pole. One new theory for the sudden warming takes a gigantic step back from our planet. This idea proposes that the ice ages were triggered by our solar system's flight through the Milky Way's spiral bracelets. Some evidence does suggest that the timing of ice ages may, indeed, have coincided with the movement of our system through the volume of stars. This passage may have been a cause for the sudden freezing—and for the warming that was set off as we passed outside the cosmic energy field. Whatever the reasons for the last great Ice Age to have eased off, though, it has not yet ended, and we are still scuttling about in its shadow.

Some 8,000 years ago, as

the ice migrated into the north, Albemarle was no longer sub-arctic. This was now a place with forests of spruce and hemlock, the sort of environment found in the Pacific Northwest, a period known to us now as the Early Archaic. These spacious towers threw aloft a high canopy down through which shafts of light would shine in shapes upon the forest floor. In spite of the carpet of needles, a few hardwoods, like oak and hickory, were beginning to appear. In the atmosphere of the great forests, an ensuing sense of place and of spirit seems to have been alive for these ancient people.

They were the ancestors of the Monacans. Their history may remain unknown to us, but we do know, from our brief contact with them, that their language may tell us how they came to be here, and illustrate some idea of how the vast extinction of huge Pleistocene animals came about. Like many aboriginal people throughout the Mid-Atlantic, their language is related to Sioux.

43

Siouan languages may have evolved just as the Romance languages separated out from the Latin. The Sioux are a western nation associated with Missouri and Montana, if not Virginia, and this suggests the first people here may have come from the west. As they migrated east, they did so to follow the game but also to move on as other bands of families arrived behind them. Their skill, like that of all modern humans, lay in a certain cleverness and perception in framing their problems in polar terms, and then resolving them with a compromise, a previously unimagined middle path. Under enormous pressures to change, they were able to leap ahead of the curve, a metaphor of sunrise, and to come east ahead of the decimation and crowding that lay behind them, the deliberately burned land and the over-hunted herds. Contrary to popular mythology, they were not as light on the land as once thought. And when an area was exhausted, they would walk on into the beauty of the morning.

The abundance that the Paleoindians pursued, as they came east across North America some 12,000 years ago, would not last. The Pleistocene was ending, and between 10,000 and 11,000 years ago, a mass extinction of the great animals was well underway. The explanations for the mass destruction of the animals include a lethal mix of a warming environment and the relentless immigration of hunters, as modern humans established themselves throughout the continent. In simple terms, it may well be that the Paleoindians came south from the Bering Strait and moved parallel to the ice sheets, always toward warmer weather and better hunting. And as the climate became too warm for the arctic animals, they migrated north into the cold, alongside the ice sheet. With the two groups moving toward one another, there had to be an encounter between them on an open plain. One family of quadrupeds may have looked down and seen circling them tiny, malodorous vertical bipeds that then threw themselves on them with a stinging fury. However the scenarios played out, within a thousand years of human arrival in North America, many of the Pleistocene megafauna were extinct. Until then, North America had presented a variety of animals on a scale like that of Africa. Mammoth remains have been found as far south as Miami, and the skeletons of camels, cheetahs, and jaguars, out west. Herds of horse vanished, as did the tapir. The first humans must have looked out at herds stretching to the horizon and thought there would never be an end to them, anymore than there could ever be a limit to the earth or sky. But they retained nonetheless in their oral tradition the story of the end of the mammoth, which they knew as the big buffalo. Faced with the plunging scarcity of game, exacerbated by arriving bands of more families, the early people of Albemarle may have found themselves in straits similar to those that had destroyed the Neanderthals.

Although the Euro-settlers had almost no contact with the Monacans, we do have an idea of how they survived here in the thousands of years after the great extinction and before the arrival of the English. This understanding is drawn from a study of the Indian tribes living today in Newfoundland. Even though these contemporary people have been influenced by contact with the outside world and by the development of the fur trade, which sustains them, researchers have calculated these allowances into their observations. And what they believe they have, as a result, is an almost pristine model that shows how the Monacans adapted to the changing sub-arctic environment and managed to survive.

Most scientists believe that they were not hunters of big game in the Early Archaic period of 9,000 years ago, an idea borne out not merely by the mass extinction but also by the gradually diminishing size of the stone points they used for hunting. As points were sharpened, they were cut smaller, as well. In the Early and Middle Archaic period, centuries before the Roman Empire, their lives revolved through the space and color of hardwood seasons, in a continuum that carried them around the perimeter of their territory and through centuries. This circle describes most of Albemarle but also includes land that falls outside its modern boundaries and extends south to Amherst County. In addition to observations made of the Newfoundland tribes, archeological research on the Thunderbird site in northern Virginia, and the Flint Run site in the Shenandoah Valley, together suggest that the Monacans would establish themselves in a base camp, then move on in rotation. In each new location an encampment would arise where they might remain for months. Imagine then, a base camp that leads off to three, four or five satellite camps, each one of which offers everything they require in a stream for water, a quarry for stone, and grasslands for game.

As the seasons changed and the game moved on their migratory way, so, too, would the Monacans, cultivating as they went the seeding of the plants they gathered but also reinforcing the vigor of the herds they fed upon. Sometime after the great extinction, they took an unforeseen path to equilibrium within this ecosystem, a gigantic mobile of balances that would remain invisible to the Europeans. And yet, as they cultivated and developed their land, they were growing their mythology as well, in their sense of lightly held mutual possession, an embrace between their creator and the land that sustained them.

Monacan camps circumscribed tracts of land amid the ice-age streams where their Clovis ancestors had arrived, and inside this rolling circle all the territory was theirs. If we know this little about them, though, experts at least speculate that the earliest campsites in Virginia may never be found. People who arrived here some 12,000 years ago may well have continued east, on to the edge of the continent. The Atlantic was low then, with so much water bound up in glacial ice. And prehistoric people would have set up their camps on the continental shelf, now beneath the swells of ocean and the swells on the boardwalk at Virginia Beach. As early groups of hunter-gatherers set their wandering distance from 70 to 250 miles, the question of why the Monacans chose to remain here has prompted a new theory from historian Jeffrey Hantman, who sees in their pattern of life the practice of their spirituality. As an anthropologist at UVA, his work in recovering Monacan village sites along the Rivanna River has been crucial in helping to bring their history out of the obscurity where it had fallen upon the arrival of the English. Although Hantman is still developing his theory, he believes that their burial mounds are next to, or nearby, the sources of copper that they believed their creator gave them. Their land, then, was inside a sacred circle.

Not far distant from their villages, they laid their dead to rest in mounds that would reach in time the stature of earthen mortuary monuments. The circle of burial mounds was a kind of language written in the texture of the earth itself. Without coincidence they fashioned a vast ring of sites that transformed the land into a landscape, a thing that speaks, endowing the hills and plains with an eloquence of spirit between the people on the earth and their creator in the sky. Hantman's theory might meet with challenges, as every new idea does, but so far he is persuaded that the evidence does link their burial mounds to their sources of copper, starting around 1000 C.E., and both seem to be in the realm of the sacred. Even so, the Monacans did not use or wear copper, though they seem to have supplied it to their neighbors on the coast, the Powhatans. In response to his question about where the metal came from, the Powhatans told Captain John Smith that it had come from a source in the west—the Monacans, who they described as barbarians he would not want to meet.

The time of the woodlands people was ending here in Albemarle. Within their oral tradition, a span of a few hundred years had produced remarkable and disquieting contacts with another wave of immigrants to the continent. Borne on the tides and trade winds of the Atlantic, a flotsam of wooden ships had been

drifting up onto Virginia shores. The Native Americans had remained within the forest as they watched the aliens from the future descend from their weird craft. On the day, perhaps, that the Clarksville point was made, English settlers were cooking in Jamestown. Pink and pious, robed in odd costumes, they brought the announcement that a queen from an unimaginable corner of the planet had set her satin slipper upon their necks, and would own this land. A century later this tribe, in motion for centuries, finally came to the blue hills and surveyed the new place where they would live. Although they saw nothing more than an uninhabited wilderness, the English themselves were not invisible. From the woods, the Monacans saw them and in their arrival, the end of their time in these valleys.

In spite of the resistance of the Powhatans, who wanted no contact with the Monacans, Smith did pull together a crew, and with an Indian guide and translator, traveled by canoe up the Rappahannock River outside Fredericksburg, and on into the Monacan territory. In the woods that day, they captured a young man, and Smith conducted an interview with him. When he was released without harm, the Monacan and English tribes remained out of contact for another hundred years. Nevertheless, Smith was able to draw a map of the unknown territory west of Richmond that showed six Monacan villages, among them, Monasukapanough. Perhaps the largest of their villages, it was settled on a Rivanna flood plain about a mile from an even earlier village site about 4,000 years old. The green field today is brilliant with the pennants of children playing soccer, and the traffic of Route 29 can be heard coughing through the trees.

The flood plain is also the site of a burial mound, and one afternoon in the mid-eighteenth century, a column of Indians reappeared in the area. They walked through the woods with a solemn intent, then left the main trail and went on to the flood plain, where their ancestors had lived for centuries. Here, they came to an earthen mound about 80 feet in circumference and maybe 10 feet high. This was a monument in which their dead were buried and in such a position where they could collectively speak to the animating spirit who had given them their lives and this land. The visitors were not alone that day but were being watched from a shadowy position amid the trees. The observer was moved by the grief in their faces and by the certainty with which they crossed trackless miles of woods without a pause or word of direction. He could not have known that they had come here to say goodbye to their ancestors, and would soon migrate, it appeared, into oblivion. Yet through his eyes, 10,000 years of humanity reach into our time. He was a lanky teen with sandy hair and freckles, and his name was Tom Jefferson.

49

THE AMERICAN W I L D E R N E S S
OFFERED THEM A ROUGH BARK UPON WHICH THEY WOULD
CARVE THEIR NAMES, FIRST AS INDIVIDUALS, THEN AS A NATION.

2

When the Europeans arrived in Albemarle, they brought with them more than the romance of landscape poetry and painting; they brought their religious ideas as well. But they established something of more consequence, perhaps, which was even then, in the early eighteenth century, instilling an irreversible shift in the world they found here. On the afternoon that Tom Jefferson witnessed the funereal visit of the Monacan hunters at their burial mound along the Rivanna, he returned home through a landscape whose composition was altering in every line beyond anything the Native Americans had known.

For the Europeans this was an uninhabited wilderness when they arrived, because the trackless means of the natives' existence left no print that they could see. Their ways of hunting and gathering, and of growing maize along the woods, were so thoroughly enmeshed within the wild, that they were indistinguishable from its luxuriance. The English and the Germans had a visible idea of what human occupation would look like, and it meant domestication. Their culture of growing crops and of herding animals fell in line with subordination rather than co-existence, and entailed as well as the clearing of forest and the plowing of land. As Tom returned to his family's farm in Shadwell that evening, loping by horseback through the woods, he would have passed the first local experiments in agriculture. These were the tobacco farms, and they were among the first footprints in the New World of an invisible colossus.

Agriculture was more than an amusing green giant, however. The advent of farming involved more than subsistence; its efficacy would braid ideas, aspirations and the landscape into a national identity. What we find in the European occupation in Albemarle is a fabric of philosophy and application whose weave still holds us together, and whose dynamic is character in action. For here was a place of self-creation that brought the displacement of others. Here was a place where entrepreneurial endeavors would be borne on the backs of people, foreign, indentured and enslaved. In this place the tumultuous notions of status and power, which had thrown off revolutions throughout history, would be set into a slowly spinning balance within the wires and counterweights of a democratic republic. History may always remain a foreign country that we can visit and misunderstand because we share so many similarities without sharing essentials, but we can nevertheless recognize in the Colonial mindset the human heart in conflict with itself. The abrasive distinctions between people of high aspiration and low achievement were often in violent play, from salacious newspaper scandal, to the glacial silence of dinner parties and the private tears of a ruined hostess. In the medium of mind and landscape, where groups and ideas formed and dissolved, the spiritual sentiments and scientific inquiries of the Romantic period would find full expression. For Tom, who came in that evening troubled yet unaware of just how much his life had been changed, the glimpse of ancient light in the world had been a crucial epiphany. And the response he would bring to the fore would shape the character and mythos of everything we call American.

What began to play out here in Albemarle in his lifetime was an appreciation for nature that arose along with our separation from it. Just as we were learning to survive on the land, we were also developing the organization that would allow us to live outside its hardships. The interstice between mind and land would pool with aesthetics and politics and spirituality, but also spark invention. As more and more people arrived here and throughout the country, what they designed was a sort of vast and intricate organization that would soon sustain many more people, in lines back across the ocean. Rather like the Atlantic rising over the continental shelf, the inundation from the east was an inelcutable event. The genius of cooperating with an unknown people toward an abstract end, to provide food outside an area and its seasons, would soon overflow the genius of living in nature and its seasons and a place. On the evening that he returned by the river, Jefferson traveled between the woods and fields, along a flood plain that lay between these two cultures.

He returned to a household and mores like others of privilege in the area. As a youth with a philosophical bent of mind, he absorbed every conversation and book whose shape gave his mind a view of limitless possibilities. Here, on the frontier, in a limbo between cultures and empires, he was keenly alive to the revolutionary thinking all around him. The Colonial intelligence had two essential ways of looking into the world that fashioned the world they saw. These were the Classical and the Romantic. The first, which arose during the Renaissance, was a mathematical and patterned view of the world. For the Classical temperament, the mystery of existence is one to be explored by reason, by investigation and quantification, a sort of architectural view of structure. The newer, emerging mindset, the Romantic, saw the mystery of existence as canvas upon which we paint emo-

tions and insights into the spiritual life, by drawing from the moods on our palette. The preferences for thinking and feeling saw two distinct yet overlapping kinds of promise before them in the landscape, if not as a platform for progress, then as place for spiritual inspiration. Their disagreements were vehement in his time, and are incendiary still. For while the Romantic may see only what is serene and inspiring, the Classical mind may see a place for new houses and roads. What Tom's father saw was land to be cleared for tobacco; his mother saw beauty. The son's ideas about land would be an endless tension and resolution between them, and would encompass the larger scope of the Colonial world. What they made here was a new land, in the sense of design and intent. The landscape behind them in England and Europe was then tantamount to parkland, a statement of great houses, class and inheritance. The American wilderness offered them instead a rough bark upon which they would carve their names, first as individuals, then as a nation.

Although he was a shy young man, Tom was not taciturn. When he came in that evening, he entered his father's sphere of personality. Peter Jefferson, the quintessential robust and commercial male, was a wealthy plantation owner, with about 100 slaves, and famous for the energy he gave off around him. With a height of six foot five and weight of about 250, Peter Jefferson cast around him a presence so large in volume and opinion that he easily dominated every room he was in. In the shadow of this monolith the stripling hung quietly. Tom may have been almost as tall but he was skinny and insecure, and given to compensating his nerdy appearance with a lively wit. Like any adolescent in orbit around a powerful parent, he would circle in toward his father for debate, and then circle out again into his own private preoccupations. His mother, Jane Randolph Jefferson, is some-

one we know little about though a lot may be gleaned from the stray few words he wrote about her. As a youth and man, Tom wrote some 25,000 letters, but only a dozen words concern the little woman who bore him and seems to have bored him all his life. Historians, like Fawn Brodie, believe that his epistolary reticence is rife with suppression and contempt; the headaches he suffered from childhood on may indeed have stemmed from various repressions, beginning with his parents' exclusionary views.

And yet he would try and resolve their politics by assessing them in the medium of the land and by using the means of self-invention as a way out of the duality. His father looked to western expansion as the future of the colonies; his mother looked fondly back to England. Peter was from an impoverished Welsh family, and was a bold, inventive and successful man. Jane came from a family of distinguished cousins in England and Scotland, who even included royalty. Here in the wild, she was something of an elitist, and nostalgic for everything English, as many of the Colonials were. In spite of the plantation around her, she seems to have felt the grandeur lost to her on this frontier.

As Peter looked West and Jane looked East, their responses to the emerging nation involved the native people and seem to have catalyzed their son's revolutionary ideas. Peter Jefferson was not just another nationalist—no more than Tom was another son rebelling against the suffocating control of the "mother country." Peter Jefferson viewed the Indians as examples of bravery and self-determination. Tom was always exhilarated, Brodie writes, by the visits to Shadwell of the Cherokee warrior and orator, Ontasseté, who came to the Jefferson house for dinner on his way to Williamsburg. The Chief's eloquence and aura, on the night that he left for England, filled young Tom with awe, and a response even more crucial: respect. From his father he learned

that the people and ideas to be taken seriously were not just the ones from England and Europe.

After his father died when he was 14, Tom lived at home with his mother until he was 27, with time out for school and politics. One night the Shadwell house burned, and he was free to marry and move to the little mountain nearby, where he had a cabin. In flux between his parents, in transit between cultures ancient and modern, he would synthesize the Classical and Romantic ideas of his world, and put them to practical use. And since he was sometimes moody, let's picture him on this night alone in his room, gazing, say, at his posters of Beethoven and Voltaire. What he had seen along the Rivanna flood plain was brimming in his mind, coming into the fore.

Tom's love for natural history was in the style of youth and of life on a frontier; his passion was not unlike our fixation with technology. He wanted to discover and understand the circuitry of the world, to count the instruments in the natural symphony whose music was in his ears for measureless hours, in the days when the mind was not compressed into a tiny space by media bombardment. He was an expansive young man and his mind roamed into philosophy for company and insight, in a bookish time when the great conversation of literature allowed those of privilege to sit outside the Socratic circle, and listen in on 2,000 years of dialectic. He may have turned to look at the books in the light of the candle. These tomes, in Latin and Greek, would have included Aristotle, where he learned the origins of biology, and understood the importance of first-hand research to explore the humming energy behind the visible screen of life. And there would have been Plato, too, whose romantic ideas of the perfect forms would have been equally appealing.

He became an obsessive reader. In law school he devised a

methodology for reading as much as humanly impossible, beginning with science and natural history before 8 a.m., turning to
law for much of the day, and ending with essays and criticism
before candles-out. One writer who engaged him especially was
the British philosopher, John Locke. In Locke he read that the
natural rights of Man included Life, Liberty and the ownership
of Property. Together, they were an inescapable triad; without
property, life and liberty were unattainable in the twilight of a
feudal Europe. And yet his youthful experiences suggested that
the formula was still inchoate, that yet another natural right was
imminent. Was the ownership of land enough? He was now in
his early twenties, a lawyer, a member of the Virginia House of
Burgesses; living at home with his mother, and reading under
his old posters. There seemed to be another idea but it was out
of focus, scintillating between the classic and romantic ideas of
his time. In the dark outside, he could hear the night sounds of
autumn, the susurration of cicadas, the murmur of cattle from
Edgehill. As he let the book of Locke's essays fall to the floor, he
caught no sounds from the hillside where today a rock quarry
throws tons of limestone dust into the pale afternoon.

On the flood plain, he had seen more than grief and loss. The
Monacan presence spoke of the ownership of land, but of a great
deal more. In those men he had seen the combinations of ancestry
and the pursuit of a certain way of being in the world, and this was
something that the Colonials were trying to accomplish, as well. If
he could see all of this, its full shape remained elusive. Even when
he rolled over and puffed out the candle, the ideas borne in him
would never be far away from his mind. His encounter was one
that he would write about years later in his *Notes on the State of
Virginia*, and seems to have become one of those foundational
moments that informed all his thinking, early and late in life.

Tom Jefferson was not the

only young man in this area who came home one afternoon from an encounter in the woods that would change his life forever. More than a hundred years earlier, another young man had a terrifying experience that presaged an invasion that he and his ancestors would not survive.

The young man was hunting along the river when he saw an anomaly and went into a crouch. Three canoes appeared in the sheet of light on the water. Although his people traded copper with the Powhatans, this was not a trading party. The men with the paddles were foreign and the individual in the lead craft was a Powhatan, whom he had seen in his village before. In the next few moments, the ancient and Colonial men of Albemarle would meet for the first time.

In the rhetoric of the day, there were "hostilities" between them. The young man was captured and interrogated for a few hours. He found himself speaking through the Powhatan guide. The foreigner said he was Captain John Smith. He asked for the young man's name. He was Amorolek. Smith asked why his people avoided the English. The answer is one Smith wrote down.

"We heard that you were a people come from under the world, to take our world from us." He told them he was a member of the Mannahoacs. His village, on the Rappahannock River near Fredericksburg, was one of several in the area; they lived within the loose confederacy of the Monacans. Also known as the Tuscororas, they were a tribe that in the 1600s inhabited roughly half of all Virginia, sharing much of its territory with the Powhatans, Mattaponi, and others. Whatever else was said between them went unrecorded on both sides. After two hours of conversation, Amorolek found himself released. The strangers went back down the river, toward the nation of the Powhatans. Amorolek, lightly wounded, went back to his river village.

On his approach, he saw the myriad trails winding in toward the village and the palisade of trees around it, a wall whose spiral design spun around the perimeter, and swung open toward him in a kind of doorless entranceway. Everyone was gathered in the open village center, and distressed by news of what had happened. He stood within a circle of everyone he knew and in the kind of deep and knowing acquaintance found today only in the commune. The arrangement of their lives gave a meaningful shape to the land.

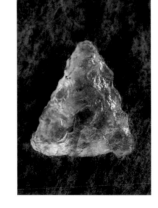

The huts formed a circle against the wall. Mats of reed were tied with dried bark to an overlapping framework of saplings, and offered small windows. As many as three hundred people may have lived in a single village. The size of a village seems to be governed by the human capacity for names and faces, which can expand outward to around 150 souls. When the numbers rise to more than double this, the first-person association makes managing things difficult and outweighs the frame of patriarchy. A society run by one man cannot have more people that anyone can recall all the time. The need then for politics arises, and here and everwhere people split off and establish new villages.

Amorolek told them that a political moment had come. Do they engage the English, continue to avoid them, or move away from this area?

The men spoke at the Chief's council. His hut was the largest and ran the length of the village. If the women in a few western

tribes were allowed to speak, that was not always the case, and it is likely that this was an occasion for the men only. Even so, each man was his own chief, in the sense that he could follow his own path in life. But they deferred to the man with the singular title because his wisdom continued to demonstrate itself on every occasion. If they deferred to him, this was by choice, and every family was allowed to move away. A man might disagree, opt to join another village in the confederacy, and take his one or several wives with him.

The afternoon was political because this was not the first

skirmish they had engaged in. The others had been with the Iroquois from the north, who had been coming into their territory, killing men, women, and children, and scalping them: trophies that would entitle the young men to declare their skill and bravery, and attain the right to speak at council. Monacans who were not killed were taken into slavery, and other oral histories allude to Iroquois cannibalism. The Monacans had also been in conflict with the Cherokee, to the south. And so the arrival of the English placed them at the tip of a triad—from which they would have to back away to find a place where they could be.

They decided to continue melting away from the English, and even the fur trappers and advance guard of farmers. They backed into the hills and eventually began moving farther south. Although Smith's famous map depicts at least six villages in this area, and more were known to have existed, they would not survive. The influx of Euro-immigration would subsume the area,

63

and by the time the Albemarle became a county, in 1743, none of the villages were to be found. Made of wood and twine, they would vanish under the mesh of grass and trees, dissolving in floods, perhaps as the Clovis villages once had eons earlier.

As he recovered, Amorolek found his balance. He taught his sons how to chip arrowheads from quartz by using the point of an antler to press carefully at an edge and pop off flakes of stone. Because they were boys, he showed them how to make small tips for killing birds. With trade between the villages and other people in the area, they thrived. His village had a cluster of gardens where the women worked to raise what they knew as the "three sisters," the domesticated crops of corn and beans and squash which were sufficient to sustain the village. His daughter worked with the women to clean the deerskins and stitch pieces of this supple material into clothing. For men and women, their styles consisted of a leather blanket that came over the head and fell to about the knees, and was cinched around the waist with a leather sash. The men also wore leggings. The women sustained commerce between tribes by weaving baskets and were known in trading routes for these, which they laced with designs of animals and flowers. In this way, living forms became abstractions with an aesthetic and spiritual appeal, and their view of the land was transformed into an artistic window onto their landscape.

The women did most of what the English would describe as the "drudgery" of hard physical labor in maintaining the village; the men would go hunting. Among their varieties of meat were buffalo, herds of which still roamed the woodlands in Jefferson's time. Elk and bear, deer, rabbit and squirrels would complement their source of meat. In the streams they threw out long cones of reeds to net fish in the current. For so much abundance in the forest, they were thankful. The men would become shamans and

perform rites in thanks to the paternal animating spirit who had given them this land and dominion over its animals.

Amorolek one day brought his sons by canoe to a sacred place, where the Monacans used to perform these rites. This sacred stage of worship is still in Free Union, not far down stream from the bridge on Free Union road. Smith's map does show five villages in Albemarle along the James and Rivanna rivers, and five more along the Rappahanack. Placing them is problematic, though, due both to the scarcity and omnipresence of archeological evidence; they seem to have preferred flood plains for a village or a base camp to which they would travel throughout the year. On this flood plain in Free Union 100 people may have been living, when Amorolek and his sons arrived. Today the warm weather brings summer campers and others to enjoy the cabins and covered picnic tables.

Close by this plain the Moormans and Mechums rivers join and run into the Rivanna. They were the ice-age streams whose waters supplied the gigantic animals and Clovis ancestors, some 11,000 years earlier. As they paddled down the Moormans, he and his sons gazed up at the sacred site. In this place where the two streams resolve into one, a rock face rises some 50 feet into the sky. The brow of stone looks out over the green depths and seems to gaze into everything else, with a sort of worn impassivity, a cold immortality with which the Romans imbued the face of Constantine. This anthropomorphic cliff is not alone. Across the water stands a natural pyramid. This great building is today overgrown with trees and brush and remains as invisible as the Mayan pyramids were in their lost centuries. Yet in the 1600s it may have stood exposed for the granite slab that it is. The two taken together, or the cliff alone, may have given a divine throne to the Mystery. Like the English on the coastal plains, they wanted a personal door to the sublime, a cathedral for splendor and a face on the infinite.

Although we know little of their spiritual life from any period contact, we do know that they worshipped a universal father. He was their creator, whose energy flowed through everything, flesh, plant and stone alike, and expressed itself around them in an indistinguishable matrix of creation, embodied in the three arteries of water. The world for them was alive in analogue and metaphor, in a confluence of spirit, land and nation. On the top of this cliff there is a stone table that communicates to the sky. Amorolek took his sons up there for the ceremony, and with other men, they may have made an offering to the force they felt moving around them.

To see how and where

the Monacan and Colonial ideas of spirituality and landscape flow into one another, we might begin with the stories the immigrants brought with them, which are symbolized by the face of Constantine. The stone face stands about eight feet tall, and yet the most monumental aspect is not the size but the significance of the imperial gaze. As the Roman emperor who legalized Christianity after centuries of persecution, he is staring into the eternal Now of heaven. This system of universal balances, of the Judeo-Christian world, is one the English felt keenly, especially as they prayed for survival. It may be hard to appreciate, but for the Colonials the realm of Christian spirituality was as actual to their minds as the texture of a stone was to their hands. To disbelieve in their dual system with its divine resolution—heaven, hell, Christ—would be tantamount to scoffing at gravity. To see the miraculous hand of God in the magnificence and intricacy of nature but then discount a divine first cause would be madness. As Plato taught the early Christians, the source of the visible

world was removed to an invisible sphere of perfect forms. And so this sense of a deep organization informing the chaos, of an unfathomable mathematics, flowed into religious certainty. The belief, embracing cause and effect, the place and purpose of humanity, was for them as scholarly and compelling as science.

When they arrived in Albemarle beginning in the early 1700s, the English brought with them their story of land and people and nation, and like the Monacan mythology, theirs included an ancestry and a creator who had given them dominion over the land and the animals. Although different in detail and doxology, the Monacan and Christian stories of inheritance travel back into roughly the same period. Around the time that the Lecroy arrowhead was made in Albemarle, another Neolithic man on the other side of the planet was having a very different sort of day. But what happened to him taught the English that the land was theirs. And the landscape they created would tell this story forever, even to those who could no longer read it.

To the northeast of the Tigris and Euphrates, where the Gihon and Pishon rivers bend toward the Persian Gulf, there lies a valley of low hills surrounded by mountains and cleft down its belly by a small river. In the distant past of about 7,000 years ago, this was a scene of flowering fruit trees and mild weather. A man, known to us as Adam, is said to have lived there. While religion teaches us that God created him, he is important to us for the opposite reason. He is the first man in the Western literary record to have discerned the presence of something invisibly alive in the landscape, and to have sensed that it was divine.

Many people believe that the first conversation worth writing down was the one held between this Neolithic man and his creator. A thousand years before the first ancient cities of Sumer appeared, he and his mate lived in a small valley, in what is today

a part of eastern Iraq. The Tibriz valley, known in ancient Sumerian as Edin [sic], has been re-discovered by an Englishman, who tracked its location out of mythology by using the cuneiform texts of an envoy, a general, and a new translation of the Old Testament. For more than a thousand years the city of Troy was believed to be mythical—until it was bulldozed to light in 1820. So, perhaps one day David Rolph's claim, that he has found the historical location of Eden, will be widely accepted. This is important to our story, because when the Europeans arrived in Albemarle, they had a sort of spiritual guidance system. In addition to all the practical pressures compelling them west, they kept alive in their hearts the mythical landscape of our oldest connection to the sublime.

The search for paradise lost informed almost all of their art. Whether in the works of the Roman poets Horace and Virgil, or in the contemporary work of Alexander Pope, their literature contained the architecture of the essential myth of expulsion and return, fall and redemption. Horace and Virgil would leave the city and escape into the countryside, and reflect in the pastoral beauty upon the soul. Behind them was the seven-headed beast of the Apocalypse, Rome, whose depredations under Nero were reaching an horrific scale in the Coliseum with the genocide of Christians, and would soon result in the city's vast incineration.

Yet before them in the Italian hills was a shepherd with his flock, a solitary youth at one in nature and with God. In the endless view of the mountains lay the tranquility of the simple life in paradise. We still frame our thinking between these polar ideas today, and they describe the essence of what is known as sin—not in the moral sense, but in the sense of being apart from the Godhead, of the separateness we feel from the divine and the meaning of life. We have tried to open doorways back to this one-

ness through art, music, gardens and landscape, prayer and meditation. In the West, this rupture between the land and the way we live upon it, this sense of sin, of being apart, appears in the story of what happened to this dysfunctional Neolithic family.

As the story goes, the sons of Eve and Adam honored their creator, Yahweh, in different ways. Cain, the farmer, offered what he had grown; and Abel, the shepherd, offered his sheep. But Yahweh, apparently preferring tradition to innovation, did not honor Cain's offering. Abel, with his flock, may have lived lightly on the land, and his sheep, by grazing and enriching the soil with manure, may have hovered in a natural balance the scope of which was ordained and ancient. Farming, for Cain, may have aroused a certain conceit not divinely favored, among angels or humanity. By contouring and changing the land, by prompting it to make life grow where none had been, and in enough quantity to feed more than himself, Cain may have set himself above nature. The gifts they offered then were of a return on God's order, for Abel, and an improvement on this, by Cain. An early tribal deity known for a sour and punitive temperament, Yahweh dissed Cain.

In a jealous rage, Cain slew Abel, and was cast out of Eden. What came next is not so often told, but still has a grasp on us today. When Cain left Eden, he became...a developer. No longer a farmer, he re-invented himself as an entrepreneur, and his first accomplishment is said to be the founding of the first city. As oblique as this may seem to us now, we have inherited the blue-

print of the story nonetheless. Deep in our culture is the idea that the city was founded by a remorseless man, and in our reaction, we have been looking for a way back to rural ingenuousness ever since.

Our ideas of the city and the country have never been the same, since that fratricide. The two ways of life still offer models for peace and antagonism that resonate with us after many thousands of years. While one brother is a paragon of honesty, the other is an exponent of cunning. One lives in communion with his Creator, the other lives in society, a world of politics. Today, we might be tempted to see Abel as authentic, a back-to-nature person with a mellow temperament and an interest in all things organic. Cain was the reverse. Picture him in power, at the center of financial meetings, telling everyone how it was going to be—before the flood. His development of the city places the urban world within the scope of everything despised by God, everything we associate with the abominations of people pushed together in unspeakable masses. His impurity led to all of that; his fall is one with the howling pandemonium of the Coliseum. Abel's purity shows what might have been our inheritance, instead, had we honored with humility our place in the divine scheme. Neither son, however, had a chance, since in both we find the natural divergence of the human river, after their parents were expelled from Eden. Upon their awakening to human consciousness, in which Eve and Adam walked out of the eternal Now of the animals and into history, which then began with a fratricide, everything that followed would be fraught with irreversibility. With such a split, a triangulating point would have to be found, a confluence, if we were to get back.

These distinctions between city and country, between corruption and innocence, and everything else we associate with them—hubris and humility, conflict and peace, pollution and cleanliness, vacuity and fulfillment—are still in play. Our desire to escape from the fruitless city and live bountifully in the country wrestles with our need to escape the boredom of the country and get to the excitement of the city. In a weird way, these distinctions are often as moralistic as ever. Every time a Developer slouches into Eden with a big new idea for the rustics, whether it's a monorail, a shopping mall, or an ice-skating rink, our collective reaction is to see him as Cain.

For the Colonials in Albemarle, there was no singular city to escape from, though many did come here from cities. For them, the Old World of Europe was an analogue for the city, a place seething with corruption and war, poverty, disease and injustice, where life, liberty and property were available to a wealthy caste alone. The sins of the fallen world were writ large in Europe by the hand of tyrants and erased by mobs, whose bloody excesses lost them all American allies. Perhaps the most bizarre parody of the Romantic desire for a return to nature was acted out by Marie Antoinette, who built a cottage where she would flounce about in costume, pretending to be a simple country maid. Pretension of this kind sickened the French, who decapitated her, and sickened also the American ambassador, Thomas Jefferson. Tom, by then

homesick for Monticello, was moved by the romantic ideal of getting away from politics and cities, and of finding a meditative path back to nature and spirit. His investigations of French architecture had inspired in him an entirely new kind of house, which would help him achieve this end.

When the Europeans came, there was no coincidence in the way they described Albemarle not merely as a wilderness, but also as one of the most beautiful "gardens" they had seen. They did have to work hard to survive, but the land would offer them an unforeseen middle path into spiritual reflection. This is still a place where the views are inspiring and in the truest sense of the word, in which a person is suddenly and wonderfully filled with awe: we sense the spirit of life moving into consciousness within us.

The Monacans were not the first to enjoy and lose an Edenic world. Rolph and his crew finally drove a lone highway through Iraqi hills, and came to the valley he believes is the likely historical location of the Garden of Eden. Seventy miles in length, and framed between mountain ranges, the valley of Tibriz is today a desert waste of urban squalor, a jumble of cement buildings and wooden shacks.

One of Amorolek's boys

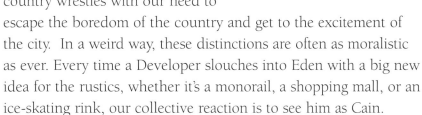

picked up an old arrowhead, which would be named a Lecroy centuries later. He looked at it, and told them it was too large—and now broken—to be used for killing birds. After the ceremony, they had come north to hunt. There was scarcity now; the

73

herds of deer were always moving on away from the human range. Their way of domesticating the herds was to pursue and cull the weakest. Without domesticated animals for food, transportation, or labor, the Monacans endured a year of privation, and the men came to this new camp. One of his sons showed him a fine piece, a tiny stone to hunt birds. The piece was so translucent, it might have been worn in a necklace.

Crows burst from the trees but no hawks were in the sky to explain their explosive flight. Amorolek paused. The stillness of the woods felt watchful. He rose to his feet. The raid was upon them. Iroquois came first with a hail of arrows and then hatchets; and this would be another skirmish in the balance against them. The arrowhead his son made was lost in the fracas there on the Blue Run plain, and began a 400-year migration along with the other, broken one, some 9,500 years old.

After the raid, they laid their dead to rest in the sacred place south on the Rivanna, where an earthen mound had been in use for centuries. When they, too, passed into history, Amorolek and his sons would be laid there to rest within the embrace of their maker; and some 80 years later, their descendants would return to pay them homage. The ending of their time in these valleys, which had begun on the day that Amorolek had been captured, was coming into its last moments as Tom watched.

When the men left the burial mound, after more than an hour of silence, they walked out of Tom's gaze and went south. They would join with the Cherokee, with whom they had had hostilities, but soon they would abandon that idea, also. In time, they would migrate north again, and join the Iroquois, where the last of their tribe died in Canada, in 1920. On the day after they left the mound, they took an Indian path marked by three chops of the hatchet, which is called Route 250 today. Not far from where they turned south, Three-Chopt Road had European buildings on it. Today, a stretch of the trail is a monochromatic corridor of brick called the Downtown Mall. If Tom and others thought the Monacans were gone forever, though, they were wrong. Their survivors were in the forest south of here, in Amherst County, where they would live outside of American history until they reemerged in the late nineteenth century. Recently, and after long efforts, they won official tribal recognition in Virginia, a status all the more difficult to attain because so little contact had left their tribal existence debatable. Official recognition from the federal government is pending.

Tom left his family home

in Shadwell, but he never left Charlottesville. Although his career often carried him out of town, he returned to the site of his early inspirations, and he tried to pass these on to others. One person he enjoyed spending time with was a boy of about seven, a local lad who looked up to him. Tom taught the boy how to survey, but taught him a good deal more than how to measure the land. Tom seems to have taught this boy, Meriweather Lewis, to understand and respect Native Americans, to pursue independent thinking.

In spite of his own confidence, Tom would fail in his first attempt to combine land and revolution. In 1769, at the age of 24, he wrote legislation for the Virginia House of Burgesses, to abolish slavery. He and his cousin, Richard Bland, who introduced the bill, were accused of treason. His mother may have been mortified by his radical behavior, but he followed the staunch models of his youth, and did so even though the calumny injured him badly. He was Thomas Jefferson then, a public man with the public name, no longer a rustic swain.

John Locke had written of Life and Liberty but finished his triad with the ownership of Property. Nothing so tangible would work for a young man who had witnessed the loss of a world in the grief of men. The pursuit of happiness was Jefferson's exclusively, the twist on an earlier idea that transformed it into something new. As with many a tiny shift in emphasis, the results were exponential: this butterfly wing would flatten the English. The philosophers he read wrote of the Freedom *from*. But the Freedom *to* was unprecedented, and can only have burst into collective consciousness in this symbolic forest of transforming encounter. An intellectual history springs to life in Albemarle, passing in an arc from the Monacans to Jefferson, through the lens of his mind and into our lives. Inspired by them, perhaps, he amplified at the tip of a quill his new idea of humane self-fulfillment, and sent this into the world as a revolutionary conviction. When he had had enough of internecine politics—so often borne of his own infighting—he would retire to Monticello, an attempt to escape Cain's society for Abel's solitude. He described this area once in 1797 with a phrase that would gather meaning as the nation grew into the new century: "These mountains are the Eden of the United States." From his aerie at Monticello he would live to see the Declaration of Independence become equal to the human desire for wonder.

When he became the third president in 1802, his sense of wonder had not let him go, and he turned to a friend who was now his personal secretary. They often ate dinners alone in the White House and talked about what wild surmise might be out there beyond the known territories. President Jefferson had terrific confidence in Meriwether Lewis, and was about to send him on the greatest adventure of his life.

HERE LAY A DISH OF LAND WHOSE VIEWS CONTAINED A CURIOUS
NEW VALUE OF L I G H T,
MYSTERIOUS AND INSPIRING. . .

3

The surf was foaming on a gray ocean.

On this apocryphal evening, some 50 years before the Crucifixion, people amid the rocks were gathering driftwood for a fire, here on the coast of Normandy. As water sizzled and ran from their feet, one of the children scooped a handful of clay that shone in the near dark. This supple and luminous chimera was utterly different from the earth of their farms, found only in the margin of land and sea, and admired for its pale luster. The child, quick with languages, called out in the new tongue of the soldiers: *"Alba marla."* She was speaking in Latin, of course; and so the name of this Virginia county may have appeared some two thousand years ago with the Roman expansion of empire.

Two thousand years later, we have the name but a great deal more has come to us than a single rib from a dead language. The Albemarle landscape reflects Native American and Christian ideals of the beautiful and spiritual, but still another tribal mythology came into these valleys and carried within its ethos an almost missionary zeal for exploration. In flowers and Maypoles, patterns of wall and hedge and field, we can discern an influence from the British islands, whose rituals ease us into a

81

dance with nature. But if these mores were provincial in origin and practice, the legends were a call to adventure. The myths of feudal Europe that came over with Colonials were a melange rich and strange; and the Latin phrase for "white earth" would convey an earlier mythos of landscape and character. Colonials found ingots of empire in the legends; and we can see just how the name garnered a new meaning over centuries and oceans.

As Rome fell through implosions and invasions, Latin dissolved into dialects. By the early Middle Ages, *alba marla* had become *aumale*, the proper name for that region of Normandy, which is still in use. If the Romans had fallen into the abyss, however, the French had not, and in 1066 William the Conqueror launched an epochal invasion of the English mainland, where he won the throne. The Norman invasion excited an inter-marriage of folktales and religion in whose offspring we can see myth, literature and landscape combine into a new sense of nationality that would play out here in the Colonies.

In the southwest of England the hills of Cornwall roll with such a resemblance to those of Albemarle that their likeness is more than atmospheric; they share a beauty and color and shape that are perfect for transplanting old rootstock into new soil. Not far from the site of the Norman invasion, tales emerged from the Welsh and Breton oral traditions about a certain fifth century Celtic chieftain, Arthur. Whether he was historical or fictional is a debate now eight centuries old, though for just as many centuries his existence was unquestioned. Most historians concede that an actual person did exist, and any of several Celtic chiefs after the Roman occupation may have inspired the myth, if not many. The monk, Geoffrey of Monmouth was the first to introduce Arthur to readers in his book, *History of the Kings of Britain*, in 1136, and he gave the uncollected tales the imprimatur, if not quite the legitimacy, of written history. Long before then, of course, Arthur had enjoyed centuries of fame for his victories against the Saxons in the early 500s, which had brought peace to the Britons after a century in which they had been beleaguered by Irish, Scots, Picts, Danes, Vikings, and Saxons. Indeed, though we may be inclined to see English history as a white monolith, for many centuries it was a melee of ethnicity, to a multicultural extent that would seem Baltic to us now.

By 410 the Romans were pulling out of England to fight Attila the Hun and other barbarians, and they left the Britons alone to contend with the tribes and invaders landing on their coast. The Britons scarcely survived. Arthur quelled the Saxons in a series of battles that brought about 12 years of peace. In his fifties, he died from his wounds after a battle—supposedly with Mordred—in 542. The peace collapsed and invasion upon invasion followed. The name of the island changed from Albion, in the Roman era, to Angle-Land, to reflect the new German owners. Britons fled to the continent for safety, but others remained in the true dark ages, without any binding sense of nationality.

Some historians believe, then, that Geoffrey, writing some 600 years later, may have invented Arthur, or elaborated on the tales, because he knew how badly in need the Britons still were for a defender, a mythic father figure in whose valor they would see their own heroism magnified in splendor. Edmund Spenser cites Arthur's signal virtue as magnanimity, and the quasi-fictional chieftain serves us because as a Celt his spirituality imbued an eye for design that we enjoy today. The worship of trees and the spirit of trees among the Celts found a cousin in the animism of Arthur's North American contemporaries; both are with us still.

More precisely than trees, though, the Celts worshipped a specific kind of forest, the sacred grove, whose space and color

and light offered a presence of the divine. The grove, further enhanced by antique literature of Roman import, would evolve into a design for the landscape whose expression would permeate English estates for centuries with an air of grandeur and magnanimity, if only through an aesthetic, and not spiritual, connection. Groves and parks would distinguish estates built in the Romantic era. They were cut in Virginia, and by Jefferson at Monticello, in part for riding. If the Colonials were not thinking of the sacred, much less of Celts, they were nonetheless using an English aesthetic to recreate a landscape of the homeland, with an atmosphere of field and forest, beneath a flickering canopy, whose lineage would trace in memory to the hills of Cornwall.

Although Arthur may never have existed in fact, the legends of his bravery found wide appeal and were retold by the authors Chretien de Troyes and Thomas Mallory. In their medieval works his deeds acquired a Christian overlay of French stamp whose concern was the quest for the grail. Early on, the grail was a simple dish, a symbol of beauty and mystery, but soon it became the Holy Grail, the cup Jesus drank from at the Last Supper and in which Joseph of Arimathea caught his blood during the Crucifixion. Legend held that Joseph had brought the grail to Glastonbury in 63 C.E., to start the first Christian mission in England. Though separated by almost a thousand years, the legends were inexorably woven together in a tapestry whose figures would represent everything heraldic and consonant with the flowering of chivalry. This was an age that saw the invention of the "gentleman," the "lady," and the rituals of courtship. The notions of divine love would mix with those of human love for the first time in the West, and they would marry as one into the sphere of the everlasting—and all in a romantic landscape dressed for the occasion.

This blending of English and French ideals moved the Celtic

sacred grove away from its position as an ancient theater and into the foreground as a new landscape of Christian spirituality. Although Eden was the landscape of signal importance, it was essentially static, a place for *being*. The Arthurian legends added the animation of an endless quest, of *becoming*. The romance and spirituality that gave rise to exploring for the sake of exploring would arrive in the New World but turn slowly secular. On these shores, a desire for divine and human love would resolve before Colonial eyes into a landscape of self-discovery. The ideal mates, the marriage of being and becoming, and all such yearning would come together in a pursuit of happiness—out there, in a romantic landscape where views of the sublime would magnify a sense of the sacred known to lovers.

The quest became its own excuse, since ending the dream invariably entailed the death of the dreamer. The pursuit of an always elusive something, of a dream for the sake of dreaming, was the first appearance in the Middle Ages of aspirations that would be called Romanticism centuries later. By the time Tom Jefferson was a boy, Arthur was an old bedtime story, read by a drowsing fire. But the idea of an endless quest would slip from the heavenly to the earthly, from grail to farm, and the mystical to the material. The value most on display in American estates would be that which an American had created for his family rather than the old value of what an Englishman had inherited. Self-creation would become the new grail, and its attainment would involve the endless frontier, found only by the dreamer.

As with all legends, of course, those who tell the stories are changed by the stories they tell; narratives impart a molding and governing effect, like parables, as vessels of collective memory in which content and design impart the message. The removal in time allows for a story to be milled in the surf of language until it is smooth and crystalline. Something like this happened with Arthur and with Thomas Jefferson. The folk tales of a warrior chief who defeated Saxons morphed into the written history of a great King who built an empire to rival Rome, with conquests ranging from Iceland to Denmark, Ireland, Scotland, Normandy and parts of Gaul. As an equal of Charlemagne, his round table of saintly knights pursued an endless quest for the Holy Grail in sacred grove and forest. Of all the medieval additions, the most important to the story of landscape in Albemarle is the way in which those who pursue such a quest are seen to embody a certain greatness, especially when a nation needs defenders and father figures. The man is monumentalized to address the centuries. His vision, imbued with spirituality, sees beyond his time.

Among the possessions in the French dowry was the name *Aumale*, which was planted in England in honor of the French nobleman who owned the land and was killed in the invasion of 1066. The English, with their own Latin influence, pronounced *Aumale* as Albemarle. The first Duke of Albemarle proper was George Monck, whose name was given to a few sites in North Carolina, if not Virginia. Monck was in the cut-and-thrust of the English civil war and helped to seat a king, yet he died in 1680 without heirs. His title fell open and was converted into an Earldom; and in 1737, King George appointed the Second Earl of Albemarle, William Anne Kappel, as the governor of the Virginia colony. He seems to have governed placidly, perhaps because he never came here. In his honor an enormous tract of land was cut from what was then Goochland County and named for his title.

As the Romantic period swept through Europe, the ancient Latin phrase for the "white earth" of Normandy, uttered before the existence of Christianity, came here with Christians, and was given again to blue mountains. Here lay a dish of land whose views con-tained a curious new value of light, mysterious and inspiring, and in whose unfolding vistas the Colonials came to see a quest still more compelling than the one that had led them here. Aspirations that diffused back through immemorial centuries would material-ize in this new landscape and be framed in language by one of their own, who inscribed the secular document with a trace of the sacred and the pagan. And the stylization of his personality into a cult would come complete with a sacred grove.

What's in a name washed ashore in the cultural tides.

Years before Jefferson wrote

the Declaration, the view West was a call to prosperity for many. The Blue Ridge frontier was rapidly evolving from white earth into white man's earth. Albemarle, growing in population and reputation, was separated out from Goochland in 1744, and given its own courthouse in Charlottesville. Albemarle in those days was huge, and included the five surrounding counties of Nelson, Buckingham, Fluvanna, and Amherst, along with por-tions of Appomattox and Campbell. The new entities were creat-ed about every 16 years, in synch with legal problems. As more people required a courthouse within a day's travel by horse, the successive counties were carved out of Albemarle.

Among the disputes that Thomas would have seen while growing up was the one surrounding the cultivation of tobacco. The crop was already known by then to destroy the land in three harvests, and the results were creating an aesthetic harrow-ing of the landscape. While the German farms may have been combed and clean, those of the English had the signs of butch-ery everywhere, in the form of stumps, and ragged fields which soon died from the nutritional depletion, of the popular weed.

The loveliness of English estates would arrive with prosperity, but in the early Colonial efforts to survive, the impressive qualities were those that evidenced the hard work and endurance of the owners. Even so, Peter Jefferson and others were the first to call for an end to growing tobacco because they felt a responsibility to pass on to future generations a landscape intact with the inspirations that had moved them. No such similar controversy involving aesthetics, landscape, and the future seems to have embroiled other colonies, and so it may be that the modern environmental consciousness now ubiquitous in the states really saw its birth here among the Colonials of Albemarle.

As Albemarle grew, tobacco was not the only stimulant growing here. Even when wheat replaced tobacco, there was more alive in the land than mere commerce. Although an American temperament was burgeoning all through the colonies, another more particular sense of our binding connections as a nation took root here. This was a mythology of place. In Albemarle, we find an American mindset that combines our inherited sense of the land and of self-discovery, which is a finer resolution of the general Yankee rebelliousness abroad. While the distrust for authority felt in the colonies is still with us, it remains essentially a negation, a refusal. The ambition to create and to realize the potential of the self, and to combine these ideas in a design for living, really does originate around the eccentric of Monticello. Here is an assertion of authority, self-ordained, the will to create rather than to negate. This becomes mythical when the passion to accomplish these ends arises from the landscape and ties a people to a particular place, endowing both with a sense of meaning and purpose. *Who* we are is also *where* we are; in the interstice is a rich dynamic of psychology.

Although he is known principally as a founding father of the republic, Tom's way of living, and the tragic circumstances of slavery which made it possible, combine in his personality the compass of our own ambitions today as individuals and as a culture. In our endeavor to use our surplus hours for self-discovery and self-improvement, we find with him a kinship that is always contemporary. To make an eclectic choice rather than simply receive a boxset of ideas was so individual an art that, as Dell Upton writes, historians trace it back to Jefferson. They see Tom as an exemplar of the first real American consumer who designed his life by filling his plate at an intellectual smorgasbord; this was unheard of in Europe and thought to reveal a lack of sensibility, a tad boorishly Colonial. It may be hard for us to appreciate, perhaps, but agnosticism like his was once considered shocking, when everything in nature stood as a revelation of divinity. In this way, Tom defined America exclusively in the affirmative, as a landscape of becoming, and this tilt toward an unrealized end would further set the country apart from older nations that already were. Here, on the periphery of empire, Tom was free to combine his enthusiasm for Native and European cultures into a fresh and bracing national ambition larger than acquisition and animated by an ancient obsession for the unattainable. The practice of individual choice and self-fulfillment would take on the form of a quest and distinguish this country irrevocably from others for whom destiny was already written.

This may be one reason why Jefferson is mythical, because we can always find in him something that is relevant to us now. For Tom the range of things we explore as a given was in full play with a revolutionary enactment of the self and society. He was able to enjoy the serenity that came from a meditation of landscape, but then switch this around to the adrenaline rush of climbing and exploring. He wanted to make a house that would tell the world who he was and what he believed in, rather than simply present the acquired taste of his age, a house that would bring him closer to the universe. He didn't want what other people had, or do what they had done; he wanted to create himself out the material of the possible. He wanted to socialize, and he wanted to be left alone; he wanted the new and the cosmopolitan, but he wanted the rustic and the authentic. Most of all, he wanted to pass his mindset on by starting a university whose instruction would bring his sort of liberal inventiveness to the conventional and conservative young men of his time. Other Founding Fathers, like Ben Franklin and George Washington, remain steadfastly in the past, antique figures in costume, static in their actions. It is only Tom, with his schizoid politics, tragic hubris, and romantic individualism, who still speaks to us today.

While many Colonials were looking East toward Europe for art, inspiration, and national identity, Jefferson was looking West. What he saw there was not just land to explore, but what sort of nation might arise from such an unprecedented potential. Although historians often see him as a Classicist, this was tacitly a romantic vision. Until the Romantic era, the span of national identity had been unrealized in Europe. People then would define themselves first by tribe, as Normans, say, but not necessarily as French. Identity on this kind of national scale would be catalyzed by the Napoleonic wars, and in the sense of a negation along old boundaries: we are not one of them, they are not one of us. In the United States, national identity would arise during the same era, and be galvanized also by wars and war heroes, and if this was exclusionary for many, the ideal would always remain inclusion. But another element would blend into our sense of identity, as well, this one from the Romantic idea of unlimited possibilities, as we transformed the natural world into a national landscape. In some part through Jefferson's own per-

sonal fascinations, we would arrive in a time of conspicuous self-awareness, a feeling of destiny on the scale of nations. To imagine the future with such a grand view was Romantic, and Jefferson's his own inspiration was drawn in part from his first experience of the sublime.

To experience the sublime

back then would fill people with sensations of awe and terror, an experience they would describe as states of ecstasy. Then and now, an electricity of universal energy can burn through human senses with the voltage of the creator and of creation. People in this moment might feel the magnitude of the world, the small-ness of humanity, and find themselves unnerved by the terror of the abyss lurking behind the visible face of things. Those of a Romantic temperament in Jefferson's time would seek out such life-changing moments in nature, storms and sunsets, glimpses of eternity. The need for such sensation may have arisen with a separation from nature and with a certain distance from the struggle to survive. The buffers of society were numbing; to feel alive again, people would reach up, to touch the face of God.

The Romantic movement, which arose quickly in the early eighteenth century, was a revolution of its own, promoting the truth of emotions over the chill rationality of classicism, which had held sway over Europe since its appearance during the Renaissance. Although both philosophies looked to antiquity for inspiration in Apollo and Dionysus—the former, a Sun God who was all calm and cool intellect; the latter, a Wine God, who was all inebriation and debauchery—the Romantics lived for the moment of inspiration. They sensed the passing of grandeur from the world, the poignancy of civilizations whose

ruins still spoke of everything that might have been; and they turned this inspiration outward to see the vast potential of what might yet become. There is little mistaking the appearance of the Romantics when the succinct symphonic forms of Mozart, say, explode into those of Beethoven. The mathematical patterns of the earlier music were swept aside by a passion of voices, weather, and humanity through all the colors of the orchestra. In the arts, the crucial change in the Romantic era was that the source of inspiration was not an earlier form of art, as it had been for centuries, but direct contact with nature, the fire of the sublime. Once there, the Romantic vision swept forward and onward into the awakening of a national consciousness, the primal character of a nation whose potential was still becoming. This was a time of vast perspectives that connected all spheres, personal to historical, in novels like *War and Peace*, symphonies like the *Eroica*, and philosophies like Marxism and Evolution. American landscape painters like Thomas Cole and Albert Bierstadt, of the Hudson River School, captured romance. Their luminous paintings of landscapes address the foreground with a shadowy space then let the view spill away into the golden light of time.

Like others in the Romantic era, Jefferson experienced the sublime and it changed his life forever. He wrote of these occasions with pulmonary intensity in his book, *Notes on the State of Virginia*, which appeared in 1787, and in whose pages he breaks from his usual reportorial prose into a passages of vivid word painting, as he describes Harper's Ferry and the Natural Bridge. These passages show an artistic mind in the way he composes and paints the view, and then transfers the experience to others so that they may feel it for themselves. The real portrait, of course, is a psychological one, but its effects were not limited to him. The

Notes achieved a great deal more than he could have imagined.

His book became the first expression of the new American mythology of place. The implicit ideas were the greatness of the new nation as embodied by its landscape, of the continuing search for the sake of exploring, and of the unlimited possibilities that belong to those who can dream of them. His ideas went to Europe in pages that combined an idiomatic American taste for journalistic detail, purported objectivity, and impassioned argument. The response in Europe was immediate; and a decade of tourism followed as citizens of the Old World crossed an ocean to experience the wonders of the New.

Naturally, a few were unimpressed and at least one visitor described the actual sites as Jefferson's "humbug." These visitors had seen grander sights in the Alps, but this was to miss the message in the medium. The purple Alp may inspire mountain climbing but they were more often seen as the ultimate defensive wall until Hannibal crossed them, and seen then as having slopes that were ideal for a group hike. The Blue Ridge, with an implicit intimacy of scale, would offer a romantic seclusion for wandering. Europeans, inspired by Jefferson's prose, came here to find the source of the sublime and to absorb its essence. The search was always shared—men and women would spend moist hours hiking into the sublime together.

The desire to drink from a well of inspiration soon evolved into visiting natural springs, where the views and healing waters were all of a piece with the grandeur. You could view the sublime and swallow the water, in a kind of transubstantiation. Springs became popular destinations throughout Virginia. Even if the view in Albemarle was not as supernal as in Warm Springs, Hot Springs and other Virginia springs where hotels were built, we nonetheless had our own annealing water. A few miles from Charlottesville, Fry's Spring became the place for a curing quaff, and soon boasted a five story hotel. In the following hundred years or so, people from Charlottesville, Washington City, and other cities would travel to the springs by horse and wagon, and later trolley car, to enjoy the waters; in fact, transportation companies came and went as a way of getting locals to the springs. As the sublime melted away from the public mind, so, too, did the belief in healing waters. In the 1920s, the Fry's Spring Beach Club was built, and the cure was transformed into socializing in the music of light and voices on water, all within a landscape.

For Romantics, nature was tamed and brought home to live politely in the form of landscape design, bowers, walks, gardens and parks. If these became too tranquil for inspiration, since they had replaced the sublime with the pretty, all anyone had to do for another rush of chemistry was to go back to nature. For many a celebration would suffice to bring nature back into society. The Maypole and the ritual of dancing around it, which the Romantics enjoyed, began with Celts as a way of bringing the animating spirit of the tree back into the center of a village. The celebrations would revive the human spirit every year, on May 1st.

Other patterns from the islands came here as well. Under ashen English skies vast rooms of stone wall, boxwood hedge, and garden give a reassuring scale and contour to the hills. The Celtic knots of Aran sweaters and ancient walls connected family and property, and arrived throughout Virginia in knot gardens, whose involutions still tantalize the eye. Many routinely share in Celtic animism with the pots of flowers they bring inside. The plants suffuse an animating spirit of life in bright rooms, casting in the sun a welter of color and scent and beauty whose effects are rejuvenating.

The Colonial experience of nature

would change our ideas of myth and literature and landscape by channeling the energy of nature into new literary forms, and the changes would ripple onward into the modern world. For the Romantic writing of the nineteenth century in the United States, the search for inspiration turns to nature but doesn't remain in poetic forms. Once here, this literature becomes something strikingly different than it had been in England. American Romantic literature emerges in the form of nature writing, in the personal essay, the solitary encounter with nature and God that is so powerful it bursts older forms of fiction and poetry. We can see this arc dramatized in the nineteenth century writers Ralph Waldo Emerson, Henry David Thoreau, and John Muir.

As their place of inspiration moves from East to West, their prose moves from theory to realism. Emerson's abstractions and metaphors, borne of the lamps and libraries of Concord, give way to Thoreau's two years of camping in the woods of Walden Pond. Even though Henry would sometimes go to Emerson's mother's house for a hot meal, he was at least out of the library. They give way to John Muir and his hardback hiking up into the blazing snows and lights of the Rockies. His prose is about what is seen and felt rather than teased out of a tiny moment and contemplated later. The actual replaces the philosophical, the robust replaces the ethereal, and the actor replaces the armchair.

As writers got closer to the thing itself out West, the works become less interior because the contact is so overwhelming that all anyone could do was gaze at the wonder of existence. Speed, exhilaration and danger stripped rhetoric down to facts—a process that was soon to accelerate along telegraph wires. Even

Twain's *Roughing It*, which is a marvel of rhetoric, is more marvelous still for the tall tales that supercede the Victorian prose and actually introduce the first examples of American cartooning.

Inspired by the West, American literature began. Hemingway may have pointed to *Huckleberry Finn* as the first American novel for its voice. But the striping down of English rhetoric to American prose began earlier, in the diaries of Lewis and Clark. As Frank Burgon writes, these diaries are in a sense the foundational American myth of exploration and return, of adventure and democracy. But they are also about the empathic encounter with the Other. And they are written in the newly emerging style of romantic American literature—a kind of new journalism.

Lewis, the stylist, and Clark, the reporter, wrote about experiences so raw that the medium of non-fiction as art entered the national mind. The events they witnessed were so powerful that all they could do was let them speak; this assertion of action over rhetoric is still ascendant. Facts that were too large for elaboration had to speak for themselves. The American landscape forced this into literature, and it began here in part with yet another of the curious ambitions of the eccentric at Monticello.

Albemarle was a jumping off place to the West. Eight previous missions, in which Jefferson had an interest, had not worked out, but by 1802, as President, he had found a way to make this one work. And the young man he sought to lead the expedition was that boy he had taught to survey years earlier, Meriwether Lewis.

He had known Lewis since the latter was a boy of seven, in Charlottesville. A bright and inquiring young man, though not formally educated, Lewis had joined Jefferson's team in the White House as an aide. They took walks together, had dinners together, and ramped up the idea of going West to discover something that would tie the entire continent together logistically: a mythical waterway called the Northwest Passage that would connect the eastern states to the Pacific ocean. They left Albemarle in 1801 and returned here in 1803; those two years would frame a modern national myth.

Much of what inspired Jefferson to endorse this mission was mythical, if not by word then by implication. His library had books about a legendary salt mountain a mile high somewhere out West; and people told him stories of having found the skeletons of elephants lying either on the ground or just under the surface. In fact, during the Revolution, he was present in the Virginia Governor's office when a Delaware Indian Chief related a wonderful folktale of the Woolly Mammoth. The shaggy animal had offended the Great Father by killing off other animals like buffalo and bear. And so the Great Father blasted the herd with lightening bolts, killing all but the bull, who fended them off with his great tusks. The bull, badly wounded, fled across the Ohio River and on into Canada. Jefferson was similarly stunned. His curiosity to learn more about these legends never seemed to let him go.

Yet from an historical point of view, he also knew that with such a mission he would take the first enormous steps necessary to unite the nation from sea to shining sea; in achieving this end he would have unexpected help from Napoleon Bonaparte.

In their own way they were collaborating toward a mutual end. Jefferson, always a canny politician, wanted a larger landscape under American control, and Bonaparte wanted cash to fight the British as well as to create a nation that would rival them before too long. When Jefferson offered to buy New Orleans, Bonaparte countered with an offer to sell the entire Louisiana Territory; and in one purchase the United States, at the age of 12, more than doubled in size. Yet, for all his political ambitions for the nation, Jefferson was still immersed in his respect for Native Americans, and his first idea was to turn the territory over to Native tribes, as a sanctuary. When the citizens of Saint Louis refused to abandon the city, though, his plan foundered. Had it gone through, however, along with his youthful legislation to free the slaves in Virginia, Jefferson might have entered history as a visionary of an almost saintly renown.

The story of the Lewis and Clark expedition has been told extensively elsewhere. What matters most here is not just the symbolic democracy of the two officers, or the interracial vote they took on the West coast, which included raised hands from York, the slave, and Sacagawea, their female Indian guide, or even the sense of a multi-racial community. What matters here, in our story about landscape, is their specific mission to interview everyone they met, and to enumerate in their journals who the people were and how they survived, and to detail the distinctions of language, culture, dress, fauna, flora, and mores. They did this at the behest of Jefferson who outlined a list of more than 100 questions that they were to ask of the Natives, regarding everything from food and clothing to a creator and the afterlife. This persistent inquiry was meant to document and understand ancient Native cultures; in his *Notes*, Jefferson laments that the Monacans had vanished before anyone had gotten to know them, and so with this mission he was trying, in a sense, to correct for the past. Spanish and French explorers had gone into the country before the Americans, but it was certainly not to take notes; Lewis and Clark were the first to arrive with pencils and attitudes ready.

A view of history through our own lens shows their mission as the first great multi-cultural embrace of everything North

American. Jefferson believed the aboriginal people had something crucial to teach us which had been lost to Colonials that concerned living in connection with the land. In addition to finding the source of the myths about salt mountains and mammoths, he meant to bring this mythology under the scrutiny of his scientific mind, by gathering through Lewis and Clark all the data possible.

The journals, in brief, are riveting.

They bear witness to brutal privation, the details of which can be surprisingly sanguinary. Tribes are routinely starved nearly to extinction by other tribes who have forced them to forego hunting and subsist on berries; the Indians they meet are universally friendly and though cautious at first, generous with everything they own, no matter how poor they are. Lewis and Clark, and their 40 compatriots, do what they can. In one instance, they kill a deer for a starving tribe, and the men are so hungry that they fall on the deer and tear it to pieces with their hands and teeth. One man eats a length of small intestine with one hand and squeezes it out with the other. Other men eat the large intestine, and Lewis cannot bring himself to tell the reader what sort of matter was oozing from their mouths. This is a detail that goes beyond contemporary imagination, and is too gruesome for the kind of polite discussion the expedition usually receives.

Nevertheless, these and other details are important to us, because they reveal an express humanitarianism that became a compelling part of their mission, in spite of the growing hostility between natives and immigrants. Contrary to the popular idea that their presence was a harbinger of genocide, Lewis and Clark show themselves instead to be a harbinger of the very kind of empathic inquiry and understanding that later inspired some-

thing called anthropology. We read in the journals of the pity and compassion they feel for the suffering they meet with; they do not dismiss or disdain or condemn anyone. Rather, they do everything they can, at all moments, to help and feed the native people, who tell them repeatedly how terrified they are of other tribes either trying to kill them one at a time, or starve them to death collectively. The French and Spanish had been contemptuous, but Lewis and Clark were not. This American encounter with the Other, then, was not always about Colonial imperialism, and should not be scored to the last tragic note when two members of the Black Feet tribe were shot and killed after chasing the explorers for miles. Long before then the mission had expanded from gathering information into volunteering to save others, yet another informing passion of the American character that rises up in response to a landscape and its people.

Clark and Lewis sent back notes on what they found, and this bolstered the President's enthusiasm to know more about the undiscovered potential out there. By then he had written his *Notes*, in which his patriotic passions are bold and declarative, and in which he writes more than painted words. He also gives a vehement if defensive exposition of everything unique and abundant found in the American continent. Written ostensibly in answer to the inquiries of Monsieur Bouffon, Jefferson enumerates the virtues of everything under his survey, from rivers in length and draw, to mountain passes, cascades and natural wonders. He is almost zoological, and whether writing at length about native peoples, plants and animals, or the temperatures of the season, the book is nothing if not astounding for the breadth and depth of his observations and implicit philosophy.

His exposition of an American mythology is not shy, either. As a writer, he is not meek or cloying. Rather, he is annoyed by the condescension of the French, whose questions and theories

presume that everything in America, its native people and animals, are small and inferior compared to those in Europe. This argument is first expressed, somewhat unbelievably, in the French assertion that Native American males have smaller and therefore inferior genitals, and from this observation they posit that the soft-handed, cowardly natives love their wives and children less, and cannot form operative societies. Jefferson writes passionately about what a lot of infuriating nonsense this is, and argues further that the natives live far more peacefully and intelligently than their would-be superiors in Europe. This is the dark side of mythology, the presumption of inferiority, and Tom's defense lit up a controversy, which was then as politically incorrect as possible. If he backed off, and defended Africans less vehemently, this may be due to his own ambivalence or his disgust with Europeans and desire to drop the argument.

What matters to us in this exchange is that Jefferson was defining America to the Europeans in a way in which we still define ourselves. The exchange is a battle between systems of belief. Jefferson's side is a new kind of mythology, however, one based upon scientific proof and accomplishment rather than upon the older European means of class and superstition. Jefferson promotes in his *Notes* a conceit that we think of as intrinsically American: everything here is bigger, faster, newer, and stronger, a point vividly made when Lewis and Clark sent him samples of what they found, among them the skeleton of a moose. Jefferson shipped the skeleton to the French, so they could relish their diminution of size.

Lewis and Clark may never have found their northwest passage, and they may have been written off in their lifetimes as something of a failure, but that became irrelevant. Jefferson was able to combine their discoveries with his own eclectic ideas, and

blend these into a sense of identity apart from what had come before. If the Greeks and Romans had given rise largely to everything European, then he was going to add the Classical and Romantic elements of his time with yet a third, which was Native American, and blend them into something altogether new, less from ambition, perhaps, than from taste. Nowhere in Europe, for example, did an indigenous culture still exist; nowhere were the tribes of Saxons, Vandals, Goths and others kept alive then or now, except in shards of jewelry in a museum case. Through his fascinations, this country would become an alloy, and take pride from its combinations around an idea rather than a tribe; for being a melange rather than merely French. The act of selecting from an array of ideas, of self-creation, would become our own unforeseen path, a way to connect the past and the future into a previously unimagined way of being in the world.

Tom swung down from his horse.

Almost everything he remembered was gone. The snarl of the trees, the wash of the Rivanna, and the hills were raucous with crows and somber in the beauty of the season. He walked about in his riding boots, heading back toward the markers that fell somewhere between land and memory, and were always moving away from him. When he was a youth, the mound had been covered in large part by trees. But was this really the mound? Less than half of it remained. Between the river and the plow, most of it had been carved away. This was no longer land but a landscape. Crops had been harvested above the dead; corn chalks lay flattened by a recent flood.

He took measurements and then began to dig. As the hours sweated by, he made careful estimates and notes. He found bodies in patterns and in layers of disarray, the foot of one skeleton thrust into the skull of another. Each time he gently lifted a skull, it would shiver into pieces. One was that of a child. Though he brought it gently into the light, it fragmented. He was moved, without telling us why, though we know that, by then, he had lost several children and his wife.

He controlled his mind by taking meticulous notes. He was an old friend of various repressions and would circumscribe the mystery with science. He would feel the emotion and desire but exert extreme intellectual control. He did some averaging, and then stood up in the afternoon light, there on the flood plain. The October warmth was passing from the sky and color was incandescing on the hills. He estimated there were some 1,000 people, at least, buried in the mound.

Although he was a Romantic in some ways, Jefferson was not a Romantic in the sense of feeling haunted, and yet he was nonetheless susceptible to the appearance in his life of a Double. Very likely by then he had taken his deceased wife's half-sister as his lover. Those who saw Sally Hemings claimed she was a pluperfect double of Martha Wayles Skelton, her reincarnation in spirit and skin, voice, form and eye. The legendary description of her as a "dusky Venus" was false. For all his suppressions of emotion, this eerie and disquieting psychology of love over death soon compelled and troubled him more than he could fathom. An appalling second chance borne of inhumane circumstances, his was the kind of obsession that would inspire Hitchcock's *Vertigo*. And so, amid the fall of leaves and light, the voices of the dead may have spoken to him across the darkening plain, and gathered momentum around his plan for sending the past on again into the future.

For this act of exploring and recording a vanished culture, Jefferson won another paternal distinction, this time as the father

103

of archeology. He now falls somewhere between the markers of memory and landscape, the connective tissue between prehistory and the American future. As he rode off that night, he traveled through a flood plain where the centuries would overlap and in less time than the colonies had been organized. Across the river, cooking fires had once lit a Monacan village for 10 centuries. And behind him, the television windows of the Carrsbrook neighborhood would flicker one day—two societies sharing the light and food and news. We are drawn to gather at night around stories that resonate into the dark.

There were lights at Monticello

whenever he returned. In the front hall, he would welcome his guests, and he often entertained. One obligation of his class was to use the front hall for instruction and to benefit his visitors by showing them some history of the area. Among the treasures on display were arrowheads and a map of territories drawn on the skin of a buffalo hide. And of the megafauna from 10,000 years ago, he had the jawbones of a mastodon, a gift from Clark, who unearthed them in Kentucky, after his trek with Lewis.

The entrance-hall feature would morph over the next hundred years and become, by the end of the nineteenth century, one of the most popular attractions available to a democratic nation: the exhibition hall. In these, specimens of history would be on display, beneath great glass canopies of light, and mingled with the latest inventions. Strangeness would abound, whether from the natural world lost to history, or from the future, as viewers glimpsed what was to become a new way of life and convenience. This contrivance would grow still further into the Chicago World's Fair of 1893, where the emphasis would fall

still more emphatically on the new and marvelous. In the late 19th century, the most popular innovation would amaze the crowd: a thing called the Panorama. Near the end of the high Romantic era, these were colossal landscape paintings in which the present moment would be enclosed within shadow and the vast western sunset would blaze with iridescence. This would be the connection to the sublime for many people in eastern cities, and one of its descendants can still be seen in the omnipresent paintings of mountains that reflect in lakes which brighten up restaurants. For most people in the nineteenth century, there was simply no other way to see a view with such grandeur, or to inhale vicariously the American mythos of the majestic landscape. With the advent of such popular landscape painting as the Hudson River School, the feeling for landscape was also a creation and response to artistic images, if not the real thing.

With a door open to the West, Jefferson would lead everyone out onto the porch with a view of Charlottesville, the University, and Blue Ridge mountains. The suffusion of light would complete the scenery, blending the civic, educational and inspirational into a uniform field of understanding and appreciation. From this height and clarity, his house would do something unique. Monticello would let nature in and open onto nature.

Like others in the Romantic era, he wanted to modify the rectilinear symmetries of pure classicism and begin anew from fresh material. He scrapped his original plans for a house, which had begun to seem insufficient to him, and turned his thoughts to Andrea Palladio, whose ideas had first inspired him as a student at William and Mary. The preeminent architect of the Renaissance, Palladio's works re-imagined and revivified the grandeur of Rome, but with a distinction Jefferson preferred over the surrounding English architecture. Unlike the Georgians

whose grand houses stood apart from the landscape as monuments to the culture within, Palladio's buildings, especially his Villa Rotunda which so inspired Jefferson, instead opened up with porticos and porches. These allowed the universe to enter as the great, unexpected dinner guest, to hover with real presence over the conversation. Jefferson's new plans for Monticello would accomplish just that. He would communicate through time, with his works in architecture as a means of travel.

The eighteenth century was an era of great novels and sea tales, and the primal adventure was that of an explorer who told of his encounters with the fantastic. As *Robinson Crusoe* tells it straight, *Gulliver's Travels* employs the same idea with savage satire. One of the popular tropes in sea adventures was that of the message in a bottle, if not as a call for help, then as a plea not to be forgotten. History has always been a message in a bottle, even if the containers of myth, art and architecture have grown opaque in the surf of centuries. The windows of cathedrals were meant to transmit holy stories through osmosis into the minds of the illiterate, as God's light animated the colors and players. And so, perhaps, light could bend through the prism of a house and through another lens as well—a university. Monticello and the University would send messages on into the future. And in the cosmology of novelist, John Barth, nations send theirs, as does the planet, an iridescent blue bottle spinning in a galactic sea.

The University was almost not built in

Charlottesville. Jefferson was able to break ground, in 1817, in Charlottesville, but only against heavy opposition from the commonwealth, which was funding the school. The landscape was at the center of the debate, even if the ostensible subject was com-

mercial growth of the region. What lay behind Jefferson's reasoning were some of the environmental beliefs he heard espoused by his father and his father's friends, which seem to have come round again into his thinking.

A committee met regularly to settle the issue of where to build the university. Several members preferred Staunton or Scottsville, because they saw potential in the former to become a gateway to the West, and in the latter to become a big river city, like Richmond. As Jefferson knew, the Albemarle area was not conducive to growth. The rivers were small and unpredictable, the roads were poor, and the area's future as a site for the satanic mills of the Industrial Revolution was unlikely.

The inability for this area to become a boilerplate was at the heart of Jefferson's plans. Just as his parents' generation had wanted to preserve a sense of the sacred for generations to come, so, too, did the former President. Precisely for all the reasons that people had to move on—because a plantation economy would not grow but a few necessary entrepreneurs—Albemarle looked like it would remain Arcadian, close enough to nature to inspire the students, as he had been inspired. As a famous man he had the power to insist, and the board bowed, though carping went on for a while.

The University has been written about in depth by many others. From the brawls between students and faculty, which ended when one student shot a member of the faculty, to the fire of October 1895 that destroyed the Rotunda but led to the university's resurrection, the early history of UVA is mostly about the louts who nearly destroyed the place. What matters most to us in the story of landscape and the University is Jefferson's particular design to capture, with the lawn's endless panorama of the Ragged Mountains, the same kind of vision that had inspired him as a youth. To soften the classical grid, he invented serpen-

tine walls, one layer of brick deep, whose gentle undulations pool the romance of the era in the gardens. And he selected an individual motif for each pavilion, which would prompt Euro-visitors to speculate at his architectural ignorance.

Jefferson was unmoved; the idiosyncrasy with which he designed both Monticello and the University were intentional not accidental. His plan was to select from an array of the past the elements that suited him. This action alone was contrary to the common practice, as people received the English tradition first, and then followed it faithfully. Just as he was lambasted by religious leaders for creating a university that did not espouse a religion, so, too, was he slighted for his agnosticism in architecture. We may see his house and university as classical in italics: an abstraction of an ideal presented to us in rows of white columns and shade trees, all bathed in an air of eminence. We may see his buildings as the grandeur of historicity—a place  where history is being historical and with the radiance of sunset. And so it may be difficult for us to appreciate that visitors in his time thought his buildings were all just a bit strange looking.

Jefferson was tired now. His house and university were not finished, and they were among the unattainable pursuits that animated him all his life. He followed his interests until he could not rise from bed only two weeks before his death in 1826. In 1817 he helped to

create the Agricultural Society of Albemarle, along with about 30 planters; their mission was to promote experiments in crop rotation, to ameliorate the ravages of tobacco. When Edward Coles, his nephew, asked him to lead an abolition movement, Jefferson demurred though he did become the group's mentor. Coles went on to Illinois in 1819 to free his slaves and set them up on farms. As the Illinois Governor, two years later, he kept slavery out of the state. Coles would die in Confederate gray, however, and this kind of ambivalence was to shape American ideas of the South. The South presented in one landscape an irreconcilable schism,

 most often embodied by Jefferson, even as he saw the horizon of civil war himself. At the age of 80, in 1823, he was in a state of high remove, in his mountain aerie, and enjoying his sense of place and purpose.

He surveyed the creation from Monticello. He enjoyed the solarium for its baths of sunlight and porticos for the height and sweep of seeming air flight over the landscape: they gave him the feel of being captain of a ship. All on broad arms far below, the Blue Ridge, Ragged and Chestnut Mountains—later renamed for their southwesterly direction—held a dish whose blue was a suffusion of inspiration. More than serene, this was a consolation of philosophy and it lay in the West.

Now he looked East. He called this "the sea view," toward Richmond, where the light is so horizontal, blue and shimmering that you might think a primordial ocean lay out there, and he did, having marveled over the shell fossils he had found on mountains. At this height, he had become a Founding Father, a celebrity in a nation that would soon see famous people as those who convey a special grace into the world. They venerated him.

And they came. The humble and curious climbed the mountain for a glimpse of the Great Man, a word or some moment in which any trace of his genius might rub off on them. Those who did know him were impressed by his energy of mind and spirit. In the summer of 1861, before the war, his neighbor at Castle Hill, Judith Rives, wrote a bitter lament in which she recalled what an unprecedented time the Virginia Colonial era had been. With the loss of Founders and Presidents, James Monroe, James Madison, and Thomas Jefferson, she predicted that something like a dark age of mediocrity would follow.

Old Tom could see the tourists but they could not see him. Although he enjoyed his hillside meditation room, where he

could see the eastern view, he spent more and more time hidden in two other rooms. These were additions with broad and black Venetian slats; and from within their shadowy enclosure he could see them looking for him. They came to see their virtues magnified and their sense of American identity enshrined in his house and landscape.

Although Jefferson sat within the bars of light and dark, neither room was a camera obscura, of course, in which light shines through a pinhole and projects a picture on a wall. As art, myth, and literature had created landscape, a new way to see and define landscape was about to evolve. He may have died about a decade before the advent of photography, but one day millions would come back and bring their cameras with them, to share their impressions of magnanimity. Photography would change our ideas of the landscape, and of the informing power of landscape, forever.

SERPENTINE

WALLS, ONE LAYER OF BRICK DEEP, WHOSE GENTLE UNDULATIONS...

4

In 1905, to relax from the pressures of his office, Teddy

Roosevelt found himself thinking of a close and pleasant location. On weekends in the woods of southern Albemarle, he found a texture of life that Jefferson had always returned for—peace unfolding far from the crowd. Rather than the comforts of a mansion, though, Teddy liked the spartan interior of his lodge, Pine Knot, which gave him a bit more comfort than a barracks. The hardwood surfaces, well and outhouse, and fires, were a vacation from the plush of the White House. What he had found was more than aesthetic, however; it was psychological; and he meant to give everyone else a chance to enjoy a similar reinvigoration of spirit.

As a child he had suffered from asthma, and his father had given him boxing lessons to build him up, physically. Even so, he remained a boy of interiors, and it wasn't until he was a grown man that he fell in love with being out of doors. The death of his first wife compelled him to throw away his career in New York State politics and move out west. There, in the limitlessness of the Montana landscape, he found surcease from his grief. But he found something else as well, which is crucial to our present experience of the landscape.

117

On horseback in the sun, he would sweat himself into exhaustion far away from the picayune and vexatious intrigues he had known back in New York. Aloft on this immersion in the physical, Roosevelt experienced a kind of rejuvenation that he believed was central to being alive and being human. In long days of sunshine and blistering in the saddle, he traveled away from everything that was merely personal and back into the consoling proximity of the divine. The cure for his depression was more than remarkable. There is no coincidence that he found solace within a sphere of mind and body and spirit, but saw something of greater value still. In nature, he felt an ebullience that he believed was quintessentially American.

As President, he became seminal to a story of landscape, because he set aside in National Parks, National Forests, and various game and avian preserves, land on the order of 230 million acres. More than preserve land, though, he established the first real venue for the worship of nature as a medium of contemplation and self-discovery, for a secular nation.

A latent paganism had emerged in the art of self-discovery and for its fulfillment a sense of place was more than crucial—landscape was the crucible in which the protean elements of the individual self would anneal with a binding agent of national feeling. What Roosevelt felt and wanted to preserve, then, was more than the great outdoors and nature, but the place where Americans were inclined to go and where transformations would happen between self and nation. In a landscape Americans were then and now inclined to see their virtues magnified, their faults repositioned, and to enjoy a vital elan of renewal. The landscape, with its harmonic field of light and grandeur, was a kind of invisible tuning fork to which Americans would turn for true pitch. The resonance was clear, distortions audible, and once in tune with

the pastures of heaven and nation, their sense of self and of belonging would be restored. This was of great importance for a country whose pieties were legal, not religious, and polymorphous, not tribal. The landscape became more than a reflective grail, or destiny of exploration, but the place where the chemistry of light and mind would enjoy a kind of bioluminescence or spirituality. As the nation grew into a vast and supple assembly, this available sphere of national feeling was important as a place where the human need to worship would catalyze millions of immigrants into an abstract sense of unity. If visitors did not feel the sublime, then pride of nation would suffice.

Nature became an unofficial religion during Roosevelt's tenure, parks, the church, and all of this was in keeping with a sensibility unique to Americans. No colony of any crown had seen nature infuse a national identity; this spiritedness is no doubt borne of a commingling of immigrant and native cultures, which Jefferson experienced keenly himself as a boy. The animism felt by Native Americans with an overlay of Christianity would fire into an alloy wholly American and the two would find sanctuary through the office of President Roosevelt. The National Park system, the first of its kind in the world, was to become the single largest outdoor cathedral to plurality sanctioned by any

nation. The culture of nature worship that Roosevelt and others enjoyed would bloom over time into a worldwide devotion to the environment.

Roosevelt may have been a powerful environmentalist, but in his time he was really in the midst of a rising wave of people who were returning to nature as an escape from the city and the mores of a tightly packed burgeoning century. The forces that made the Albemarle landscape so appealing were an amalgam of art, literature, technology and war that would drive people into an idealized past, rather than an idealized

future, to find a sense of national identity. Those earlier ideals, of an agrarian Romanticism, had helped inspire the Civil War. The rejuvenation felt by Roosevelt's generation was a reaction, in part, to that war, and their desire to preserve the landscape involved a profound need to rescue the springs of inspiration.

The south flew into the war

on a sentimental tradition from Europe, embracing the homeland as the ultimate cause. National identities in Europe were then on the rise in the galvanizing heat of the Napoleonic Wars. The American identity was still young and fragile, however—not as old in 1862 as movies are today. The political containment field of the Constitution could not hold the polarities. Southerners believed that their sense of identity, arising from the landscape, was more profound than a merely political conceit. Theirs was a view back into the chivalric past of England and Europe.

The soldiers of the north marched in step with a modern sense of nationality that would see the various regions grow into an overarching super-state. Their landscape was often urban and industrialized, and what they brought to bear was practicality over feeling. In spite of early and steady victories by the south, where feeling held sway, northern factories would produce more materiel than an agrarian landscape could match with idealism. As Sherman destroyed the landscape, its beauty would no longer inspire those who saw more delusion than reason in the cause.

After Reconstruction, Albemarle languished. The future went west and north, and in a spirit of isolation, the south was left out of the nation's industrial boom. The area of Albemarle had never been a site of action during the war, with the exception of a skirmish on Rio Road that was led by George Custer

against rebels, just on the west side of what is Route 29 today. With the exception of the Woolen Mills, at the end of Market Street, which made white coveralls for slaves and then confederate uniforms, there was otherwise not enough going on here to warrant a concerted union effort to destroy the town or its economy. The very Arcadian ideals that had made this area so difficult to make a livelihood in, and turned it into a doorway to the west, had come around to spare it throughout the war. The area simply didn't merit a battle.

After the war a new form of art changed the way the north looked on the south. The images of the holocaust would set the scene, the place, and individualize, rather than monumentalize, the dead. Photography would pique a taste for revenge against the south and investors punished the area by sending big industry elsewhere. Arcadia would remain arcadian, as payback. And the evolving new images of the southern landscape would go on to bear strange fruit long into the next century.

Of all the people who photographed or otherwise memorialized the battle scenes, the images of Matthew Brady became the most famous and persuasive, in the way they connected the war to southern fields. His images of the dead strewn over a blasted landscape were surreal, and stripped the gloss off Romanticism. Just as Lewis and Clark had finally let the facts speak because rhetoric diminished their impact, so now would this uninflected medium speak in the direct manner that Americans liked. Paintings had shown Greatness on Horseback, king or general with chin high, and raised steel, in scarlet flamboyance. That would change. Journalistic photography would instead look over the ground and show what things were really like.

The result was to change the American ideology of landscape. In the wake of the war and of Brady's images southern

122

Romanticism was consigned to the past and the Virginia landscape became its reliquary. From then on, the American future would draw personal inspiration from romantic landscapes but national inspiration from the abstract new horizon brimming in big business. The place to explore lay not in the sunset but in monopolies. The corporation would challenge and engage the genius of organization with the same fervor that was still driving others to pack up and move west.

At the century's close, a raft of miraculous inventions—the car, electric light, telephone and airplane, to name a few—came racing at people with the speed of modernity. This technology reshaped our experience of time, distance, velocity and landscape. A train ride of 13 miles an hour, for example, would leave people giddy with astonishment and amazed by how their view of the world was altered. People felt the acceleration all around them, and began turning to the past, where timeless values were intact and offered them a meditative stillness. Jefferson enjoyed an enormous vogue as nineteenth century Americans sought him out as the original visionary of national identity. Possibly as many as 40,000 to 50,000 people a year were visiting Monticello at the century's turn, even though it was the home of Jefferson Monroe Levy. One such tourist was Roosevelt on July 4th, 1901, a visit that may have allowed him to find and buy nearby Pine Knot. With a shrine as the epicenter of the America, the surrounding landscape would soon offer up its intangible beauty.

As the culture accelerated toward the looming century mark, the mountains and cerulean evenings of Albemarle gave those who came here a feel of something eternal. History could be found in a landscape that evoked the earlier romantic nostalgia for the greatness that had passed from the world. But rather than elicit a desire for exploration, the landscape would fulfill a desire for a personal connection to history. A similar diminution appeared in the fine arts, as well. The picturesque replaced the sublime, and the grandeur of landscape paintings made room for the intimacy of engravings, most famously by Currier & Ives. Tourists found here a combination of the mythical and the picturesque—of the grand but also of the reassuring. As monuments and monumental landscapes will, visiting the past also offered communion with an invisible majority of the dead, whose presence for Victorians was palpable and always powerful.

Once it was fixed in the past, Albemarle came into the present; its future would lie in its history. Tourism became the new agriculture and beauty, the new crop. This quiet rolling interior spread out before the mountains would supply an atmosphere of frayed Romance through old estates at the end of cedar avenues. Albemarle became something which it had never been while Jefferson was alive, and which it was only able to attain many years after the conclusion of the Civil War: the seat of American history. As England had been for the Colonials—the true north of a cultural compass—so, too, would Albemarle become for Americans. Once merely lovely, it now became a landscape of national magnetism. Such magnetism would need protection.

One of the first Americans to feel this pull from afar was a man from New York, who came here in 1834 and took a tour of what was then the hulk of Monticello.

Lieutenant Levy alighted from

the carriage and walked upon the lawn. Although he had never met Thomas Jefferson, he was one of the deceased President's most vehement admirers. As a Jew who had suffered years of anti-Semitic abuse in the U.S. Navy, Uriah Phillips Levy viewed the separation of church and state as a clause that would not only protect religious minorities but also establish an unparalleled country. He wanted to create a place of remembrance, and, as Marc Leepson writes, he may have been the first person to see the house not as a property of the moment but as a shrine to history. Given the discrimination he was enduring on his ascent in the Navy, he was sometimes afraid that the crucial separation, and its author, were being neglected.

On his tour that day, Levy found a mansion that had suffered. The owner before him was James Turner Barclay, a local pharmacist who had tried to create a silkworm fortune on the estate when he bought it in 1831. In the three years of his ownership, Barclay wound up cutting down most of the grove of oaks and elms that had been planted by Jefferson. The Barclay family claims their ancestor did try to preserve the house, and that his nefarious reputation is well undeserved. The Randolphs and Jeffersons who saw and heard of what was going on up there, however, were furious. They viewed his industry as contemptuous treatment by an owner who supposedly despised Jefferson. Levy found a place plundered of possessions and plantings by pilgrims. Even then the curious came relentlessly to see the house and grounds, and often took something, if not for outright utility, perhaps, like fire wood, then for a souvenir, some little icon to transmit a tincture of the famous spirit. After a wrangle, Levy bought the estate with 552 acres, for $10,000, or about half the asking price. In its state of soft collapse, Monticello may have been a picture of grandeur but it was darkened nonetheless with a certain Gothic aquatint. A shrine may have two sides.

Even before Jefferson had begun building Monticello in 1769, readers had begun enjoying novels like *The Castle of Otranto: A Gothic Story*, by Horace Walpole. The house in Gothic romance becomes a principal actor in the story by embodying the sins and virtues of the hero. The psychology of light and dark embroils the house as an analogue of the monstrosity or nobility of human conceit, and shows the world a conundrum of endless speculation. The human soul lives on in the architecture in a sort of ghostly transference, whether the house is actual or imaginary—the House of Jefferson or the House of Usher.

When Jefferson wrote the Declaration, at the height of the Enlightenment, the idea of a quest for spiritual grace in nature inspired Colonials. But soon, and borne on the emerging Gothic sensibility, another quest would capture popular imagination in those years and now, and this would be an exploration into the dark. One writer, especially, began to change our ideas of landscape back when he was a crumpled little freshman at UVA.

In the winter of 1826,

only five months before Jefferson lay dying, a little man named Edgar Allen Poe, with dolorous eyes and greasy hair, went out one morning for one of his walks. As a drinker and gambler, he often took long walks, possibly to help burn off the toxins in his system. On these rambles, he followed his inclinations away from the social lights of the village—the province of the short story—and into the forest, which has always been the proper setting for tales and adventures, which offer encounters with the strange and supernatural. For hours he would sit on an outcrop in the Ragged Mountains and brood until day had died away into nothingness and his fears were manifest in the enclosing forest. Although he was only enrolled until the fol-

lowing December, having remained one month short of a year, Poe was inspired by the Albemarle landscape. Many people today still feel an apprehension for a certain kind of landscape that traces in part to the defining works of his genius.

In "A Tale of the Ragged Mountains," his hero becomes lost in the mist of the "wild and dreary" mountains southwest of Charlottesville. In a tale that blends hallucination, out-of-body experience, and past-life recovery, all induced by morphine, the young writer establishes a signature piece in which nature is not a theater of the sublime but of the supernatural, not of benevolence but of menace. He may in this respect have foreshadowed the existentialism of later European writers, because his view of nature was not of the Divine Architect, but of random entropy. And so it may be no surprise that he fell into a swoon over the easy death and decay of the Great Dismal Swamp of Virginia, whose melancholy twilight became an analogue of southern slavery for other writers, like Harriet Beecher Stowe and Henry Wadsworth Longfellow. If their views were ostensibly moralistic, though, Poe's were not; his nature was an unplanned and inexplicable universe whose only real effect could be to arouse terror.

The two views of nature held by Jefferson and Poe could not be more antipathetic, and yet their similarity appears to lie in the emotional register of the person on the quest. On his first visit to Natural Bridge, looking over the edge gave Tom vertigo and a serrated headache. He later bought the bridge for its scientific mystery and as a triumphal arch of the sublime. Far below and away we find Poe with his Dismal Swamp. Inspired by the swamp, and by the mesmerizing allure of rot, Poe would see in the morass of chaos everything uncanny and macabre, a taste for which would twine slowly up from his corpus and grow into our time. What is crucial here is a view of a landscape either as a place of creation, and self-creation, or of decay and death.

Many Americans, then and now, prefer to see a landscape in which the sublime appears with a star-spangled clarity, the red, white and blue of Justice and Freedom for all—as an ideal, if not an attainment. They prefer to look up. For others, reality is often harrowing. They see addiction, melancholy, and obsession. If Jefferson's view seems corny and hypocritical to some, Poe's has enjoyed instead a twentieth century popularity through embellishments of his fixation with looking down. If Jefferson could not look down, Poe could not look up. Since we are naming fathers here, we may see Edgar as the Father of Goth. And a new Gothic view of landscape traces to his inspiration in this area.

A story of landscape is invariably about how a sense of place can shape a regional, and even national, sense of identity. With the entrance of Poe, we start to see something new. If Jefferson's landscape is somewhere, then Poe's is *nowhere*; the dread of his characters arises from their losing their sense of place. If God is all existence, then nowhere has to be supernatural, and the step from the one into the other has to be toward self-disintegration. As the new century guided us away from farms and into cities and then into a sphere of mass media, our collective sense of place began slowly eroding. Poe's void has seeped into the corporate landscape through various styles of modern architecture.

Although another 100 years would pass before Poe's vision would exfoliate into mass popularity, his vision would become pervasive. In recent years his dread of the forest has translated through popular entertainment into our own modern dread of bland industrial space and corporate warehouses. These zones exist outside of towns as forests once did, and it is into their unknown depths that characters now wander into trouble. The shared laws of society, back in the village, are somehow lost or

abandoned upon entering this weird nowhere of forest and complex. In film and television, the omnipresence of corporate landscapes is paralleled by the olive-drab hills of the California chaparral, which often appears as a universal location for America. The result of these influences, in design and entertainment, to say nothing of development, is a subtle erasure of the regional and particular. The meaning that a landscape may endow in the creation of character gives way to an emptiness in which media shape behavior. A dislocation of identity, and the void that may ensue, can fill with a new medieval dread of the unknown—the secret and supernatural forces of the Internet and government.

As the second millennium drew near, people in town spoke of the secret government listening-post on Peter's mountain and of the apocalypse coming online, all on a feedback loop that runs behind the walls of culture to an outlet in Poe's Ragged Mountains. Although few nowhere zones exist in Albemarle, the site where Poe would sit and daydream is still out there, on an outcrop of stone overlooking Ivy. The psyches of Jefferson and Poe reflect radically different inspirations, and diffuse into the American zeitgeist. This ink blot exam separates those who see progress from those who see devastation, even in the same view of houses going up on an old farm; the view often depends on the lens. There may be no coincidence, then, that Jefferson's views appeal to those in a bright landscape, while Poe's enshroud those within the radium glow of the urban dark.

By the end of the Victorian era,

most people coming to Albemarle would opt for a Jeffersonian outlook of limitless optimism, the very sort of ebullience which Roosevelt enjoyed and which expressed a national temperament. Conservation was their theme, and in the agrarian views of

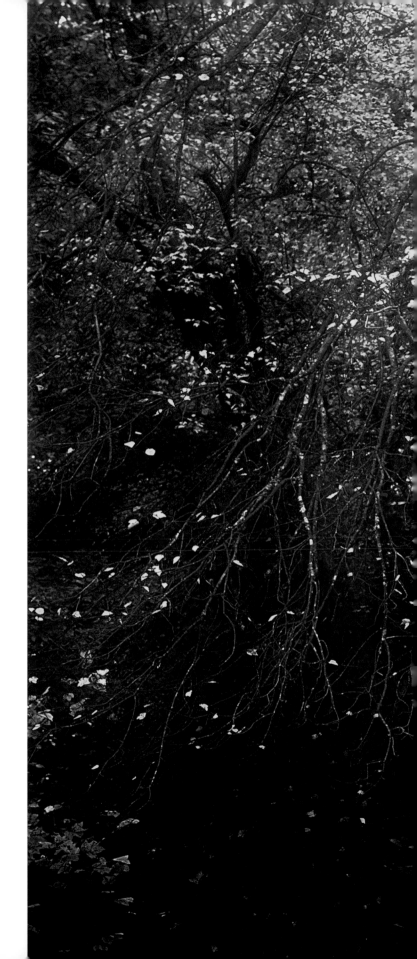

Albemarle, they would see a connection to a Utopian way of life that Jefferson believed in. When Uriah Levy bought Monticello, then, in 1834, what he saw was inspiration in the landscape. In the plains below, estates that were English in design and plantations by economy roamed the view as far as he could see.

Among the families who amassed and designed plantations were Thomas Walker who built Castle Hill, the Coles who built Enniscorthy, Coleswood, Cloverfields, and others. Other early names include Carr, Minor, Via and one Shiflette. Among the Colonials were the Rives, Randolph, Cabell, Venable, Maupin, and Jouet families; there were thousands of others. What visitors could appreciate in a visit, say, to Farmington or Estouteville was a view without the smoke and dark of the industrial revolution that was rumbling in the north.

The Albemarle estates often feature designs in boxwoods in an English manner in which rooms are created for privacy outside. These were the places for secret gardens and romantic scenes. Boxwood rooms, with perhaps a small bench, a pond, and encirclement of flowers, would offer a suitor an opportunity to make love, which in the parlance of the day meant an endearing declaration or attention. Other kinds of fences were made, from tree stumps to gathered stones, and even now it is not difficult to find stone walls arranged, yet crumbling, on an inexpli-

134

cable path in what appears to be an unused track going nowhere in the woods. The deep groove of the roadbed reveals the action of carriage wheels, and an invisible yet breathing pursuit.

The nineteenth century saw a new way for people to enjoy the landscape. Rather than appreciate its beauty from the calm of a picnic blanket, people began creating sports whose play would send them into nature with an exhilarating rush of speed and through a dimension of light. These sensational effects would find a modern equivalent in roller coasters, but early on, and now, people here would follow an English style of life. They would go fox hunting, which is popular today as much for the gossip, it is said, as for the jumping and galloping. The baying of the hounds on a cool morning, the electricity of roaming the coloring fields, are bracing. And many on the hunt prefer, of course, not to capture the fox, either, for this is a quest whose goal is rejuvenation.

The event known as steeplechasing began as a race between church steeples. In the spring and fall, here in Albemarle, we celebrate our own harvest and planting festivals with steeplechases at Foxfield and Montpelier, and horse shows. The landscape presents an extravaganza whose chief event is socializing.

We find a space whose pressure restores a gregarious pleasure to life and one that we seem to favor under open skies.

For those who rode in the cavalry, and others who loved to ride, one way to stay in trim was to play polo. The games played inside a sandy ring at the UVA polo center, or out upon its field, can translate some idea of what an actual cavalry charge might have been like. The excitement is more than tonic; the rush is catalytic; you feel an adrenaline burn in the explosive power of the game. There, in the dusk of old mountains, beneath the buzz of lights and insects, the glow of evening feels timeless and deeply alluring, as it gleams with the luster of everything now.

Among the most pleasant of the invented pastimes was the practice of standing people around a diamond and then racing through a pasture to chase a ball. The pace and measure of baseball were in keeping with a century whose days moved around a turn of the planet, and whose afternoons would allow us to share many lives in one event. We come together today around town for a communal few hours in an invented landscape. Games of softball light up the night in the public parks. Teams and individuals row along the Rivanna Reservoir. The University venues contain roaring crowds whose alchemy transforms UVA's Scott Stadium into a descendant of the imperial coliseums of Rome. All of this

compression of people and energy leads to a maximum point of transference after which we leave the experience feeling changed by the vast diffusion.

The landscape is the stage on which the community gathers to refresh itself. The more public the location, the more in tune we are with the hierarchy, and those locations call forth the characters we play on those boards. In nature, though, in the chaos of a structured game, we can lose ourselves utterly and return with fresh nerves. People come alive to each other. This was the experience Roosevelt found for himself in the west. And in the truest sense, this is a vacation—i.e., vacating something—and of letting something new rush in. The beautiful views of Albemarle would send a flowing spirituality into the empty space, in a kind of respiration between a landscape and those who give themselves to it completely.

The landscape was more, then, than a backdrop for the poets. It was a medium for transformation. Beyond aesthetic inspiration, as Roosevelt understood, a landscape would allow everyone to find a sense of rebirth. All we had to do was find a way into the view, and while sporting through ample sunshine, we found a way to swim in reservoirs of light.

Others, though, preferred taking a picnic to Monticello. An amenable host, Uriah Levy welcomed those who streamed

up to Monticello so often that he rarely had any peace; but he always invited them in for a tour, welcome, or not. His renovations were lauded in the local paper, as well as his patience with so many people wandering all over the property. Those who had seen the house in the last years of Jefferson's life would lament over the state of disrepair it had fallen into, but Levy would rebuild and refurbish until his death in 1862. His relations fought over his will and the house was closed for 17 years; the caretaker was very lax. When Jefferson Monroe Levy, a nephew, finally wrested the house free of lawsuits, he arrived to find the mansion so ramshackle, that it had fallen into a state somewhere between ruin and relic. And as his uncle had done before him, Jefferson Levy repaired and opened the house. The house was already a shrine, though what visitors took away was not a spoon or candlestick, but what it meant to be American.

In spite of his hospitality,

and then because of it, a campaign began in 1901 to take Monticello away from Jefferson Monroe Levy, and it all began when he opened his doors one day on Maud and Martin Littleton. They were in Charlottesville to see the University on their way back to New York City, where Martin had defended Harry K. Thaw for having shot and killed Stanford White. The shooting was infamous, and White was the renowned architect whose works had shaped the UVA grounds. At the far end of the Lawn, where Jefferson's inspiring view of the Ragged Mountains had called to Poe, White placed Cabell Hall—thus entombing the Lawn, as Poe might have seen it. His restoration of the Rotunda after its fire also won him wide acclaim. With these invisible degrees of connection between them, Levy and the

Littletons spent the afternoon together. As Mrs. Littleton later testified before Congress, her reaction to Levy was nothing personal. She found him very nice and attentive and full of information about the house, and his restoration was admirable. And yet, as the afternoon wore on, so, too, did the presence of the Levys, rich and powerful Jewish New Yorkers. Jefferson Levy was nationally famous as a Tammany Hall Congressman, financial tycoon, and Wall Street speculator. Newspapers loved him.

As they said goodbye at the door, the accumulation of everything Levy, paintings to furnishings, began to weigh upon Maud, and she told Congress that she felt as though the national shrine had been taken over by "a rank outsider." By the time she testified in Congress, Maud had ramped up her distaste into a national campaign. As a New York socialite she was connected, as was Jefferson Levy, the stylish New York City millionaire, and so, once again, those from the north were in a brawl to control the American past and its springs of mythos—here at the shrine within this landscape. But Congress decided not to buy.

And Levy would not sell. In fact, years earlier, an ex-Presidential candidate, Williams Jennings Bryan, had written him asking to buy the estate for the public, and asked Levy what price would suffice. The answer had been on the order of, not for all the money in the national treasury. As a former Congressman, Levy, too, testified before Congress, and told them that he had spent about one million dollars in restoring and then maintaining the place, an expense exacerbated by vandals and visitors alike. Even as he was testifying about his summerhouse, as many as some 50,000 people a year were going on sojourns to Monticello, in search of some connection with Jefferson and his spirit.

So great was this national movement that Levy joined the Thomas Jefferson Memorial Foundation as a vice president, when the organization was founded to raise money for the Jefferson memorial in Washington, D.C. Yet, the weight of ownership soon began to oppress even an irrepressible owner, who finally put Monticello on the market in the early 1920s. By 1923, the Thomas Jefferson Memorial Foundation came up with the half-million dollar asking price, in 1924, a few months before Levy died.

After 89 years of the Levys' devotion to keeping Thomas Jefferson's house as a shrine, it was finally going to become just such an institution, and leave the realm of the personal for the marbled halls of the historical and monumental. The estate would become a symbolic pinnacle of American aspirations, sending a transmission from the past, through Jefferson, on into a limitless future. Many would come to the mountaintop mansion to announce their ideas for the future, and many of these visions would present a whole new way of saving the American landscape as the final monument to national consciousness.

The 1920's saw an enthusiasm

sweep the country for all things in nature, from joy riding, to exploring, to preserving national lands. While some of this had attained an official status with Roosevelt's creation of the national park system, many were looking simply to get out of the city and back into the refreshing cool of a breeze, and to swim in a stream on an August day. For others, nature writers like Muir and Thoreau had been great inspirations. And still others were drawn to explore for themselves, having seen the great panoramas of western views that were open for public showings in the exhibition halls. One group, who loved the romance of old houses and gardens, organized themselves into the Garden Club of Virginia, in 1920. As activists, they organ-

143

ized fund-raising tours of Monticello, and netted $7,000, or $70,000 in today's valuation.

Their momentum carried into the current Historic Garden Week in Virginia. In the last week of April, as many as 250 historic houses and gardens open to the public; the money goes to restoration. One such project was to restore the East Range gardens at UVA.

If the ladies of the club were

concentrating on the intimacy of gardens as a landscape, the men in the boys' club were thinking on a scale suitable to the male ego. Around the time that Roosevelt took office in 1901, two congressmen, from Tennessee and Virginia, tried to create a national park in the Blue Ridge. The plan meandered until 1925, when the site was set in Virginia rather than North Carolina, and the double intention of saving nature and growing tourism dollars came together in Shenandoah National Park, which borders Albemarle. The first views of Colonial inspiration would join the informal catholicity of nature worship, and soon become accessible to everyone.

And yet, when landscape is the prize, the denouement often turns upon displacing people. The park would not open until 1935, due to imbroglios surrounding the mountain families. The Commonwealth swept them off the map by condemning their property, thus settling the price of land, and fears of potential speculation schemes. The resulting lawsuit to protect the mountain people reached the U.S. Supreme Court, but it refused to hear the case. Many moved away, some were resettled elsewhere gratis, and still others were evicted and had their houses burned. In the end, some

465 families were moved from Blue Ridge land where they had been for generations.

Before the park could open in 1935, the Civilian Conservation Corps, or C.C.C., built the Skyline Drive. The corps was one of President Franklin D. Roosevelt's high-profile solutions for unemployment. A contingent of 1,000 boys and men, who worked in the park under the supervision of the Army, built the highway and put in hiking trails, fire trails, towers, picnic areas, amenities, stone walls, cleared forest and planted dozens of new species of trees and plants. The natural environment of the land eventually disappeared, and a new one took over. Nature was transformed into a landscape. The park is, by design, then, a garden dressed as 200,000 acres of wilderness.

In the 1920s, Americans jumped into their Model Ts and began to enjoy a new and instantly popular form of recreation in the boom—going for a Sunday drive. By foot and by automobile, Americans began exploring the environment. The way they did so changed the relationship with landscape—and a sense of the tranquil and serene was soon superceded by the new rush of speed. The sensation of racing on horseback, which was limited to one or two people, could now be shared by an entire carload of hilarious revelers. One person might seek a view and isolation in nature. And others might enjoy carrying a party off toward the sublime, for a picnic and procreation.

The county then had muddy roads that swung at an easy pace through the scenery. Their meandering paths still offer us today, though, what they created for the Colonials. With nary a straight line, the Albemarle roads send the scenery into motion. Nature comes across as a living thing through this animation. In the twentieth century, the first highways gave people this experience of racing with a landscape, and it was one of the century's

early wonders. The landscape runs alongside the car every day.

America, racing in roadsters, began enjoying in the 1920s its first experience of youth worship, and what the youth wanted was to be outside and free and wild. Theirs was an intoxication of youth, whose effervescence was not just the champagne and bootleg whiskey, but the boundless sense of going up—everything after the war was newer, faster, and better. Into nature came these bohemians, absorbing sunshine into every pore. For decades women had bleached their skin, but the flapper was not her mother. Inspired by the swashbuckling movie star, Douglas Fairbanks, Sr., who always had a tan, everyone would have one, and sun worship became enormously popular. In search of nature and love, people would find romance in the outdoor rooms and privacy of orchards and vineyards.

Although artists and writers and bohemians were coming to Albemarle back then, the area was largely agricultural. In the 1930s some half a million apple trees showered windfalls over the countryside; we now have 35,000 apple trees. Royal Orchards, which dates to Jefferson's era, earned its name through the popularity of its apples in the courts of Europe. The roads were still muddy, though, and in spite of almost 100 years of newspaper editorials clamoring for

paving, very little improvement was seen. In the time of the building of Skyline Drive, this was an area of vertically integrated farms that were self-sustaining, whose crops fed livestock and family, which then went to market, along with milk and eggs. As the markets specialized over time, though, so, too, did the family farm, a result of which has been experiments in wine grapes. Although Jefferson could not make his vines produce well, many others, beginning about 15 or 20 years ago, planted vineyards; their success has helped Virginia wines rival California's. The orchards and vineyards together have drawn designs, and the flowering trees and vines have been among those that enhance the earliest ideas of the garden.

Few Albemarle farms today can sustain the earlier style, however, and though there are vast operations for bison and beef cattle which cover the view to the top of a hill, beneath storybook clouds, these are now in the minority. The 750 or so farms today often shelter more taxes than cows. And even though many fields are growing suburban houses, the area remains mostly undeveloped; 60 percent of the land is covered with trees. In late summer, the county fair blazes with rides and brilliancy, and the displays of agriculture and livestock draw thousands to see a life more historical than con-

temporary. There, within the timeless embrace of the mountains, the fair presents a way of life that is now subsiding and blooming into something altogether new.

What is new, of course, is the dominance of the town and the suburbs over agriculture. In Charlottesville, Court Square is the apex, there on a hilltop whose height and centrality reinforce the supremacy of the law. Landscape essayist, J.B. Jackson writes that these squares were common, and the idea of having a courthouse in the center of the square may have come here from Europe, where triumphal arches and monuments often symbolized an anchor to a noble history. Most towns were laid out in grids, he writes, and Jefferson designed the nation's capital as a grid, which made the city's designer, L'Enfant, laugh. The grid, while of classical origin, also came from the National Survey which Jefferson authorized as President. In this survey, much of the state and open land was laid out in a grid for the convenience of making a survey, and the grid of a town, then, was a microcosm of this. The grid was meant to use the design of landscape to ground reason in people—straight lines equal straight thinking—and to encourage the emergence of an agrarian utopia whose people were virtuous citizens. Jefferson hated cities and so this was his idea of creating an ideal democratic nation, of

small landowners and democrats.

To the north of Court Square, the important nineteenth century houses appear in a stately sequence, and in these properties the real romanticism of the century is evident in gardens, box hedges, and mature shade trees. To the west of the square is Lee Park, named for the general. Within a frame of churches, a library, synagogue, funeral home, and historic society, the park radiates quiet. To the south of Court Square, we roll down hill into the domain of business, along Main Street. There, at the eastern end of the Downtown Mall old brick buildings watch the commotion of people attending festivals of music, literature and film. The ghosts of another age call from the facades in fading ads; one in Art Nouveau script shines on for "Delicious" Coca-Cola. The paint broadcasts the silence of cotton and tobacco commerce that went on at the old rail road station. The brick structures now house blond wooden floors and stylish companies, and the old CSX train company that built the Belmont neighborhood now brings visitors.

Over the years the downtown and university areas began growing toward each other and the result has been an overlapping of business and neighborhoods. Areas of light industry are now embedded in neighborhoods. West Main Street is one of these, an old gasoline alley that was once outside of town and that is filling in from the edges with an infusion of restaurants. This hybrid economy evolves as new ideas grow into old structures. Indeed, there are several old gas stations where you once might have pulled in for an oil change, and today can buy a designer sandwich instead.

As the ideals of the Roosevelt era had arisen from a reaction to the Civil War, so would these new ideals emerge from WWII.

In the 1920s and 1930s, romantic ideals began turning monstrous in Europe. Ideologues pulled Romanticism inside out, and empathy with spirit and land-scape turned into urban industrial ferocity. The fashionable new barbarism grew from the war ruins of Romanticism, and Lenin, Mussolini, and Hitler hearkened back to the glory days of motherland, empire, and chivalry borne of a landscape to which their listeners could turn for sentimental proof. Some kind of mass seizure was underway; as agrarian Oligarchies morphed into industrial republics, tyrants pointed into the past for a virulent new nationalism. In the United States, the last malignant flourishing of chivalry, led by brown shirts in bed sheets, helped pour the cement and set the iron bars for the jail cells of the future by altering for many a sense of des-tiny and landscape. The American totalitarians were also inspired by a sense of place, not from paintings or poems this time, but from the newest of media, movies.

In 1915, D.W. Griffith brought a sensation to screens around the country in one of the most significant films of any generation. In his movie, *Birth of a Nation*, the director seized upon the romantic and chivalric traditions of Arthur but twisted them around into an heroic representation of the Knights of the Ku Klux Klan, and the imagery sparked a

revival throughout the south. In the summer of 1925, when the Scopes trial was going on, the national Klan held a rally in Washington, D.C. Although the Klan had all but disappeared, enrollment soared after the movie. Some 25,000 members, in hoods and sheets, marched in the nation's capital, and with their avowal of a grand tradition, they shared with European totalitarians a sense of identity borne of a defeated landscape.

One of the terror cells in the march came from Albemarle, and in previous years there had been several cross burnings, and one bombing, in addition to a large Klan march on Main Street, with Klansmen speaking at the county court house. It might be reasonable, then, to suppose that African Americans sought to be invisible. Those who had been freed before the civil war, but did not leave the state within a year, faced recapture. For an indefinite time some of those who were free lived in hidden villages throughout the woods of the county, perhaps on the old flood plains where the Monacans had lived for so many centuries. The sites are gone though they did leave headstones now enclosed by a century of hardwoods. In the woods today, not too far from the enclosed graveyard of a prominent family, you can sometimes find a lost graveyard of slaves; the stones are among the lost fabrications that tell the human story of our presence, now tilting in the forest mulch.

African Americans held onto the landscape and the town. In the 1920s they held parades and parties. The Vinegar Hill neighborhood was a thriving community of stores and shops and restaurants. Of the more than 3,000 local farms in the '30s, many were owned by blacks whose farms were admired. As whites left the land in the depression, blacks remained, unwilling to leave the landscape of their ancestors. In the 1930s, as the Klan dropped any pretense of merely espousing

religion, it faded in this area. And yet, though the races seem to have gotten along well until the school integration battles of the 1960s, landscape with its claim on the past, and its design for the future, would came into play dramatically.

In the mid 1960s, during the school integration battles here, Vinegar Hill was razed. The bowl of land, whose buildings were by then dilapidated, was scraped flat. As a sign and cosine of future livelihoods, though, the area was not rebuilt with stores that black or white entrepreneurs might open, with apartments, or with a way for people to nurture the landscape. Much of the hillside was paved with asphalt. While half of this space today is vacant, the other half offers fast food restaurants, the unemployment office, and a few small businesses. This has been a national trend—to knock down old buildings, vacate neighborhood ownership, and fill in with service arenas—and some may see in this the first footprints of globalization. Such a design would seem to offer few entrepreneurial opportunities without an inheritance of ownership and the culture that supports such enterprise.

As the engines of commerce

had built armies for world conquest, so now would the same engines make communities. The growth would appear largely in Charlottesville. Scottsville, on the James, White Hall, near the Blue Ridge, and Crozet, would remain mostly unchanged. American prowess and power would be turned to an immense effort in nation building throughout Europe with the Marshall Plan, and here in the United States, in planned housing. The first of these developments was Levittown, Pennsylvania, and for all the abuse it receives for aesthetic reasons, another quality remains. This is the perfection of sameness. Those who had

fought in the war, and felt its shock, wanted a landscape the design of which created a sense of rest, quiet, stability, and, above all, predictability. For most of the 20th century, life had been catastrophic—war, genocide, collapse and poverty on an international scale that presaged the death of nations. On the high of victory and recovery, American know-how was going to get rid of the nightmares, forever. Think of the hedgerows of England and France transplanted onto American soil, but with all the suburban advantages. And in the kind of partnership for the future that the 1939 World's Fair had promised, the task would be undertaken and achieved by the visionaries of futuristic American corporations.

This new landscape was built for the car and for an unprecedented level of mass consumption. For all the Dads plowing the yard with a lawnmower, Moms happily planting mums, or kids floating on swings, the landscape of Kodak would vanish. The new landscape would fill us, but leave us empty. And a famous person from Washington would come to Monticello to address the nation and announce the cure.

As on official shrine, Monticello

was the place where, in 1965, Lady Bird Johnson spoke to the nation. The American highway system had opened vast tracts of land and became the greatest interactive art installation in the world. Many people thought nothing of throwing bags of garbage out the window, however, and the margins were fields of trash. The First Lady's idea was to seed flowers in the medians and to outlaw littering. Her campaign to Keep America Beautiful succeeded, in part with a commercial depicting the tears of an American Indian. She received a shock on her way

to Monticello, though, as she traveled through an endless corridor of billboards.

Jefferson's pursuit of happiness was becoming the pursuit of satiety. If the former was always unattainable, for those after the Second World War, the attainment was finally going to happen. With the deployment of cars into a landscape of shopping malls, everything would be at hand. The result some five decades later is a raft of issues that have all arisen from this mesmerizing new landscape that shimmers along highways. If billboards are no longer the issue, then the effects of this changing landscape are. Rather than the nowhere of Poe, this new landscape is a cornucopia of the mythical garden. Many of those who decry development may be among those who have forgotten the scarcity that has left an imprinted desire for abundance in collective memory. Foreigners from developing nations, though, tend to be amazed.

This landscape, this commercial enterprise zone, morphs rather like a vast and invisible gelatin dome, and we travel in a circle around this area like the Monacans of another time. Shoppers enjoy themselves in a created landscape as others enjoy an actual landscape, and a perfect purchase can intoxicate—as Jefferson knew while on his own compulsive shopping sprees. The emotional undertones of this environment even reach into the spiritual by issuing a lush and musical and lighted simulacrum of something like a shrine, in a garden of plants and water under a Jeffersonian skylight. Here, the pursuit of happiness is supplanted with anything imaginable, for belly or soul, an appetite of hunger or for self-creation. The promise of the 1939 World's Fair—a future of plenty—has come to pass, with unforeseen complications.

Beneath an oculus that showers light softly over us, we can participate in a latter day search for self and individuality and all

in a corporate landscape. All of the astonishing excess in a shopping mall casts off its own lights and socializing energy and becomes for us a world in which we spend many hours, when the parking downtown, and in the rain, is a hassle. Even if these commercial zones are found often on the edge of the forest, they are now a creeping corporate kudzu that twines in through windows in the wires of televisions and computers. This new landscape has a perimeter that circles the sofa, drives to the golden arches, drives to the shopping mall, and ends, after so many years, in a drive to the hospital. The division implicit in the serene suburbs that were built after the Second World War has borne fruit in a myriad of health problems, all within an enclosure that extends almost everywhere and whose interior and exterior design are infused with media. If we sit at a light, talking on the cell phone, the kids may be in back, watching cartoons. Our great achievement of comfort can separate us from the landscape, of moving vitally through it, as Roosevelt knew.

In reaction to the sprawl of this new landscape, some have sought to control development. And in this area, the development along Route 29 North remains buffered in green. In spite of the giant constructions on the edges, few parking lots open directly onto traffic, even though this is an environment for the car. And 29 South is still a picture of early Albemarle, exhibiting the past for all those looking for rural quiet. Still others look to engage with nature directly through exercise and exploration.

Our future is our past, and to understand the complexity ahead, we have to see the landscape somewhere between the polarizing lenses of Jefferson and Poe. This is an area built on a plantation economy, and many who came here had to move on if their services fell outside that economic

umbrella. In the 1920s and early 1930s, people with power made a decision to cease from luring industry here and concentrate rather on tourism and in the preservation of the area's beauty. That decision framed the landscape we enjoy, but its future will continue to swing upon the vagaries of economic decisions.

As the Albemarle area flourishes, it faces the same issues of congestion that have transmogrified Northern Virginia. Many are concerned that such sprawl is coming to this area, and yet growth here may be curtailed by the economy, a pale descendant of plantations evolving through an array of people and companies within the shade of the historic colossus, UVA. The decisions made at the University direct the future of this landscape. While in the last 20 years or so, other universities have grown research parks, UVA has sought to grow big sports revenues. The University has emerged into world class status and constructed new campuses for its schools in business, law and medicine, but these remain insular affairs and the graduates leave because the white-collar bandwidth is so narrow. A few research parks have gone up, but this is not a Research Triangle, and the boon to business and traffic remains largely an influence of alumni and tourists. Whether the University decides to license sports or intellectual property in the future is the issue. Between the economies of big sports and big research there lies a world of landscape.

Some people would like to control the future by containing the past. One result of this has been the wide appearance of conservation easements, which place land under protection from development, almost all of it for perpetuity. This landscape has become a subtle new monument and may some day join the network of official nature trails in Sugar Hollow and the Rivanna

walking system which encircles the city. A paradox of the automobile age is that views open to those on horseback are less accessible to those in a car. County roads are often conducive neither to biking or walking, much less parking. As the area grows, then, perhaps some of these views will open with trails, so that more people can follow their Jeffersonian instincts into these vast reservoirs of light. Land and light may be invisible as wild gardens but they are the final expression of what began with Jefferson—to have a home where the pursuit of happiness ends, in this world. The beauty that inspired him may remain Arcadian and ours, and for as long as the states shall stand.

We come here for the energy, people say, for an implicit rejuvenation of self, and we gather in Albemarle the same way we collect in a kitchen at the start of a party, to create enough pressure for some meltdown, a fusion through voices and laughter of many people into one moment. If we see in the landscape a refraction of spirituality in prisms and facets of topography, then the undeniable action of light upon the eye is at work; and the landscape becomes the film upon which we may develop a sense of who we are. The action is more than metaphorical. Studies have shown that an effect on neurochemistry can be achieved through prayer and meditation, as the mind's spatial awareness expands out toward limitlessness. Such a personal confluence with the ineffable is one that Andrew Newberg describes as a state of Unitary Being; in some way the mind attempts to close for us the gap that opened in Eden. This mystical experience is one whose rarity may be available to many through the popular avenues of Romanticism. The effects of beauty, light, and land may all lead, then, to something like a metaphysics of landscape. And so our compulsion for con-

servation may entail our survival in ways that we cannot even now fully realize.

For many, the call to be here is audible and people often find an incomparable area in which to live and raise a family within the hues of inspiration. The elusive center remains the landscape, and in a secular way we express our connection to the land through a variety of symbols we may scarcely notice. A certain sartorial swank may represent the utility of a farm, or the Anglophilia of an estate. Some may attest to earnest politics from a palette of colors in moss, clay and cork, or to the sunnier affiliations of cream, coral and cobalt. Jefferson once did something like this—seek the authentic, the land, and a rush, all within a sense of self and nation. Whatever the style or manner we use, the understatement is the same—a profound sense of identity which arises from our sense of place. As an infant learns to see itself through its parents' animations, so may we see ourselves in cathexis with nature. The meaning and purpose we feel through daily fluctuations with the landscape around us, as we drive, walk, and live, sustain, and may even help to create, our spirit.

Whether through a connection with the past, or with our better selves, we often seek to experience what Jefferson felt when the light of the past and future lifted him for a single, transitory moment out of himself.

Perhaps a psychic awakening is always looming for those who feel the living allure of what is beautiful and possible, who respond to the neurochemistry of light, motion, art, and self-creation. In this awakening, we search for a new connection with the intangible, with an embraceable love.

One summer evening, an old dirt road led me through an evergreen door and into a hidden grove. All around me in the cricket-sounding stillness, the trees and tall grass were tranquil. A stream purled between a brace of boulders and the sunshine beneath the cedars shone in bronze coins on the lichen-green and blue-gray surface of stone. The sound of water over stones, the elusive smells of fresh-cut hay and honeysuckle, and the occasional few fireflies all eased into a lingering impression of other evenings. This was the vesper hour and transformations were taking place. A fallen cedar looked like an elegant woman doing the backstroke in her pool, a pair of lavender flowers became her lost dinner gloves, and from these simple points a story came to life. She had fallen in during an uproarious midsummer night's party and was swimming to encircle and hold onto her lover.

Here in the dusk was a memory of love disguised as a meadow. And so I went on, following the soft curves into the evening and into all the landscapes that lie ahead.

BIBLIOGRAPHY

Olsen, Steve. *Mapping Human History, Discovering the Past Through Our Genes* Houghton Mifflin Company, New York, 2002.

Poe, Edgar Allan. "A Tale of the Ragged Mountains" *Complete Poems & Tales.* Vintage Books, New York, 1975. 694

Upton, Dell. *Architecture in the United States.* Oxford University Press, New York, 1998.

Frazier, Sir James. *The Golden Bough, A Study in Magic and Religion.* 1 Volume Abridged Edition, The Macmillan Company, New York, 1951.

Doveton, Frederick and Ralph E. Griswold. *Thomas Jefferson, Landscape Architect.* University of Virginia Press, Charlottesville, 1978.

Brodie, Fawn M. *Thomas Jefferson An Intimate History.* W.W. Norton & Company, Inc., New York, 1974.

Muir, John. *The Yosemite.* The Modern Library, New York, 2003, Modern Library Paperback Edition.

Caras, Roger A. *A Perfect Harmony, The Intertwining Lives of Animals and Humans.* Simon & Schuster, New York, 1996.

Harbaugh, William H. *The Theodore Roosevelts' Retreat in Southern Albemarle: Pine Knot 1905-1908,* Reprinted from the *Magazine of Albemarle County History,* 1993.

Wittkofski, J. Mark and Theodore, R. Reinhart, eds. *Paleoindian Research in Virginia: A Synthesis,* Special Publication No. 19 of the Archeological Society of Virginia, 1989.

Reinhart, Theodore R., and Mary Ellen N. Hodges. *Early and Middle Archaic Research in Virginia: A Synthesis,* Special Publication No. 22 of the Archeological Society of Virginia 1990.

Reinhart, Theodore, R. and Mary Ellen N. Hodges, eds. *Late Archaic and Early Woodland Research in Virginia: A Synthesis.* Special Publication No. 23 of the Archeological Society of Virginia, 1991.

Reinhart, Theodore R. and Mary Ellen N. Hodges, eds., *Middle and Late Woodland Research in Virginia: A Synthesis.* Special Publication No. 29 of the Archeological Society of Virginia, 1992.

Kelly, James C. and William M.S. Rasmussen. *The Virginia Landscape: A Cultural History.* Howell Press, Charlottesville, Virginia, 2000.

Leepson, Marc. *Saving Monticello The Levy Family's Epic Quest to Rescue the House That Jefferson Built.* University of Virginia Press, Charlottesville, Virginia, 2001.

Moore, John Hammond. *Albemarle Jefferson's County,* 1727-1976. University of Virginia Press , Charlottesville, Virginia, 1976.

Bergon, Frank, ed. *The Journals of Lewis and Clark.* Penguin Books, New York. 1989.

Newberg, Andrew, M.D., Eugene D'Aquill, M.D. Ph.D., and Vince Rause. *Why God Won't Go Away Brain Science and the Biology of Belief.* Ballantine Books, New York, 2001.

Duncan, Dayton, and Ken Burns. *Lewis & Clark An Illustrated History The Journal of the Corps of Discovery.* Alfred A. Knopf, New York, 2002.

Orvell, Miles. *The Real Thing Imitation and Authenticity in American Culture, 1880-1940.* University of North Carolina Press, Chapel Hill & London, 1989.

Jackson, J.B. and Ervin H. Zube, ed. *Landscapes Selected Writings of J.B. Jackson.* The University of Massachusetts Press, 1970.

Rosenblum, Robert. Introduction. *The Landscape in Twentieth-Century American Art, Selections from the Metropolitan Museum of Art.* By Lowery Stokes Sims and Lisa M.Messinger. The American Federation of Arts Rizzoli, New York, 1991.

Ambrose, Stephen E. *Lewis & Clark Voyage of Discovery.* Photographs by Sam Abell. National Geographic Society, 1998

Howatt, John. H. Introduction. *American ParadiseThe World of the Hudson River School.* The Metropolitan Museum of Art, New York, 1988.

Shenandoah National Park. www.nps.org

Historic Garden Week in Virginia. www.loc.gov

Geoffrey of Monmouth. www.britannia.com

Monacan Indian Nation. www.Monacannation.com

A Brief History of King Arthur. www.hallofnames.com

174

ACKNOWLEDGMENTS

We were extremely fortunate that so many wonderful people helped us in so many ways, out of a shared passion for the beauty of Albemarle. In somewhat chronological order, Babette Thorpe and Cathy Link of the Piedmont Environmental Council helped us early on by calling and opening doors for us. Many people spent hours enthusiastically showing us the land and telling us its history: Peter Hallock, Woody Baker, Greg Graham, Peggy Augustus, Tony Vanderwarker, John and Mary Scott Birdsall, Michael and Lynn Levine, Tony Champ, Bessie Carter, Carter McNeely, Venable Minor, Jack Fisk and Sissy Spacek. Others gave us free roam, including Coran Capshaw, Dave Matthews, Felicia Rogan, Luca Paschina, Edgar Bronfman and Jan Aronson, Halsey and Deborah Minor, Linda Wachmeister, Jim and Bruce Murray, Jr., Cynnie and Mike Davis, Janice Aron, Jim Phelan, Beth and David Sutton and Mr. and Mrs. Paul G. Burghardt. Hal Young's history and arrowhead collection were invaluable. Jeffrey Hantman's conversation and lectures provided wonderful information about the Monacans, and his reading of the Monacan chapters was extremely helpful. Roger LeClare gave us a presidential tour of Pine Knot. Jim Riddell, extension agent, lent us a wealth of agricultural history, Josh Albert helped by wrangling buffalo. We also thank Alison Dickie and Ruth Hart of *Albemarle* magazine. Anne Browne of Foxfield and others of Garden Week, Monticello, Ash Lawn-Highland, and Carter Mountain Orchard were kind enough to let us come out and make pictures. Jill Summers graciously invited us out for a morning of horse and hound, and Florence Wilson let us wander among the sheep. Loring Woodriff spent a day guiding us all over the area, and John Lanham set us loose for kite day. Much gratitude to Bobbi Grant Llewellyn for her insight and help with picture editing and book production, Dawn Hunt for copy-editing and fact-checking the text, Tom Jehn for reading the final manuscript, Richard Chenoweth for his architectural acumen and Kitty Chenoweth for her editorial wisdom, and Katherine Cox for scanning and preparing the photographs. Luca DiCecco assisted on location and Jon Golden assisted with production and computer technology. Also assisting on location were Cara and Jenna Llewellyn and Helen and Emma Emory. Without the commitment and vision of our sponsors, though, none of this might have happened. Chief among these was Mark Giles of VNB, enthusiastic from the beginning about this project and in building our sponsor network; Eliza O'Connell, working with him, was wonderful and cheering and generous, as were Anne Hooff and Douglas Camp of Keswick Hall. Steve McLean and Jim Faulconer inspired us to drive every road in the county. Margareta Douglas led searches in the forest for lost graveyards. Kim Briehl piloted her plane for aerial views. Jerome and Paula Beazley met us with cool wine at sunset and Kakie Brooks brought her love of the arts to our ideas. The insight and advice of Dorothy Batten Rolph and Robert Strini helped to awaken ideas. One sponsor, Cary Brown, came on in the book's embryonic moments with ideas, books, help and encouragement. We owe her an immeasurable debt for such strength of heart, to have seen what was possible out there, in the landscape.

PLACES

ALBEMARLE

Copyright 2003 Albemarle Books

Text Copyright 2003 Avery Chenoweth

Photography Copyright 2003 Robert Llewellyn

Published by Albemarle Books
885 Reas Ford Road, Earlysville, Virginia   22936
434.973.8000
www.AlbemarleBooks.com

Book Design by

Michael Fitts, Avery Chenoweth and Robert Llewellyn

Printed and bound in Singapore

First Edition

Library of Congress Cataloging-in-Publication Data

Chenoweth, Avery.
   Albemarle / words, Avery Chenoweth ; photographs, Robert Llewellyn.—1st ed.
      p. cm.
   ISBN 0-9742707-0-9
   1. Albemarle County (Va.)—History. 2. Albemarle County
(Va.)—Pictorial works. 3. Albemarle County (Va.)—Description and
travel. 4. Landscape—Virginia—Albemarle County—History. 5.
Landscape—Virginia—Albemarle County—Pictorial works. 6. Jefferson,
Thomas, 1743-1826. 7. Monticello (Va.) 8. Indians of North
America—Virginia—Albemarle County—History. I. Llewellyn, Robert,
1945- II. Title.

   F232.A3C47 2003
   975.5'482--dc22
                              2003013913